Lived, Loved, Laughed

The secret to no-regrets living

Pamela Jean Steele

Contents

Contents

Introduction

James Joyce wrote 'They lived and laughed and loved and left'. Do you dare for this to be on your epitaph?

It was when I was called to attend the scene of a suicide involving a leap from the top of a magnificent marble, deco style staircase that I decided to write this book about facing our worst fear - death and in doing so then making the absolute best of every moment we have on this earth.

This tragic suicide powerfully illustrates just how precarious and fragile human bodies and minds can be.

So unprepared are we for sudden death or a serious attack on ourselves, whether it be by suicide, accident, illness, abuse or terrorism, that we are often completely devastated by it.

Emily Craddock, Greenpeace activist, to whom this book is dedicated, tragically died at the age of 27 whilst on a dangerous mission on the Amazon. Her mother was so traumatised by her tragic loss that she died of cancer a couple of years later.

Yet Jemima Coulthard, age 102, lost her son and, despite immense grief, decided to get on with loving life. On her last birthday she attributed her longevity to being happy and content (Northern Echo Aug 2010). I believe she wholly accepted, unlike most of us, that along with life comes its shadowy partner - death.

Alan Watts looks at life and death as part of a game of polar vibrations of existence, where one has to win over the other eg light over dark or sound over silence . He believes that, instead of playing the game of winning we should accept each polar vibration equally. So then we could accept the inevitability of death as much as life.

Perhaps, as a result of this thinking, as Nietzsche, the German existential philosopher *of the early 20th century* states, you could '**Say Yes to Life**' and '***Dare to become what you are or who you are***' instead of being scared of its shadowy partner - death. He believed that, as we grow up, we seem to become more consciously divorced from our real selves or our real drives and wishes. This is perhaps due to childhood conditioning, social circumstances, religious beliefs or many other influences.

Trauma, art, psychotherapy, meditation or hypnotherapy can all give us flashes of insights into who we really are and what we really want in life.

I have found in my work, as an Incident Recovery Psychologist, that traumatic experiences can often awaken people towards knowing themselves better and wanting to live a more meaningful life.

Survivors or witnesses to critical incidents such as the 9/11 and 7/7 terrorist attacks in New York and London, or the shocking suicide I have just related, spoke to me, not just about the horror of the event, but also of suddenly having a clearer view of their own lives. As well as experiencing many normal post traumatic stress reactions, such as feeling overwhelmed or confused, many experienced a shocking insight or awakening into their own existence and mortality (existential shock/awakening). Often they didn't like what they saw. This shock then catalyzed them into taking action to dare to move towards living, loving, laughing and being happier in a way that they wanted.

Through re-examining their lives with me, some decided to change their jobs or even their partners, whilst others decided to go travelling around the world or work for local or international charities. Most decided to look after their own health more and re-examine their general life balance so that they could begin to live and love life in a happier and more meaningful way. This phenomenon, we call Post Traumatic Growth.

Some books guide their readers towards happiness through them learning the value of pleasures, satisfaction and excitement. Other books guide them to happiness through the reader understanding the value of wisdom, authenticity and integrity; through the value of having positive, loving relationships and through accepting themselves with purpose.

My alternative approach, whilst leaning towards the latter, is to shock my readers (whether they be lay people or trained psychological professionals) towards happiness through writing about tragic and traumatic accounts from survivors and witnesses.

I present a selection of true stories from my clients (with altered names and circumstances for the sake of their anonymity) who have survived near death/ traumatic circumstances or who have been touched by another person's sudden or accidental death. I also present other tragic stories that have already been in the public domain.

Then, whilst briefly awakened I take my readers on a psychological, philosophical, biological and spiritual journey from *'being strangers to themselves'* to knowing themselves better and recognising and doing what they really want in life and then daring to achieve it. **To dare to live, love and laugh**.

I take them on a journey towards identifying:

- Who they are, who they want to be and how they may dare to aim for this
- How they can seek lasting, positive, loving relationships
- How they can become truly happy, from within, in the way they want
- How they can escape their own hell, in terms of the personality they have become, the lifestyle they have created or the hell of their own human chemical needs and desires
- How they can adhere to a faith either in a higher being or in themselves
- How finally they can ensure that the actions they want to take, will happen
- How they can then further their happiness and enlightenment through helping others

I have always been fascinated with death since the age of 11, when just before my grandmother died, I heard her saying that she had never really enjoyed her life. I was shocked at this statement and vowed never to be in that position, at her age, or at any age. About a year later, the *Aberfan* disaster happened, where many Welsh children, of similar age to me, had died in a mudslide that had engulfed their school. This had left a whole town totally traumatised and bereft. There had also been other major incidents that had had a large impact on me as I grew up. The IRA terrorist bombings, particularly the Guildford pub bomb, where I had been at University, had shocked me as does any terrorist activity even now.

In **chapter 1**, through reading about real life tragedies and valuable philosophical perspectives, my readers can begin to understand how life and death go together, just like light and dark or sound and silence. Also how this can help us decide whether we lose the game of survival or whether we want the freedom to live, love, laugh and be happy for as many moments of our lives as possible. Understanding then how the possibility of this freedom can give us anxiety enough to run away from it. I present the ancient Ten Commandments as a way that God, I believe, helped our ancestors run away from this freedom through curtailing their darker human urges. I then dare to suggest that the groups of Ten Tips I give in my chapters might be more appropriate than these Commandments in that they help both to curtail negative drives but also to encourage positive drives. Whilst still grasping this desire and dealing with the ensuing anxiety, this chapter then helps us look at what we REALLY want in life and who and what is important to us.

Chapter 2 looks at further tragic stories where we see how, often out of pain, people faced their anxieties about grasping their freedom and began to dare to live. By looking at daring personalities such as well-known sportsmen and how they dared to lose to win we may begin to see how we can dare to live ourselves. Also we look at our many selves, the good, the bad and the ugly and how we can embrace or change them as we want. Finally looking at our obstacles to daring and how we may overcome them.

Chapter 3 de-mystifies the pain and joys of love through stories of rape and rapture. The different types of love are explained such as falling in love, platonic love, object love, celebrity love and deeper love. Factors for successful relationships are highlighted such as similarity amongst partners despite men and women possibly coming from different planets. But also equality and getting the right amount of dependency is important. Finally important tips are given on improving genuinely loving relationships.

Chapter 4 looks at what happiness is and how suffering can then temporarily destroy it. We look at different types of happiness and use Elvis Presley as an example of someone who pursued hedonistic pleasures to the extreme. A different kind of happiness is then given by the Dalai Lama, Buddhist leader and author of books on this subject – one which is gained through wisdom, understanding, authenticity and integrity; through having positive, loving relationships and through accepting oneself with purpose. Happiness is further explained sociologically, psychologically and biologically. We then look at how happiness is pursued through satiating our bodily needs from food, alcohol or drugs. Or how happiness can be gained through a healthier and more positive means such as music and dancing, play, love, humility and compassion.

Chapter 5 reveals how, despite the seemingly simple ways of daring to live, love and laugh, we often make our lives our hell. It looks at the personalities we may have developed, through growing up, such as being too chaotic, being too much of a perfectionist, being too compliant or wanting to please others or being too strong, or controlling. It also looks at the nature and devastating effects stressors, both within us or at work and at home, can have on us.

In **chapter 6** the tragic public suicide already mentioned, highlights just how fragile our human body is. Until we are forced to realise this we can easily assume that we are invulnerable to accident, illness or worse death. This chapter gives us a comprehensive but simple manual of the workings of the human being so that we can take as much care of ourselves as we do with our cars! Giving ourselves an annual MOT, consuming fuel that helps us run well and taking ourselves out for a good run to keep all our parts running efficiently is as fundamentally important to ourselves as it is to our cars. We then look at how we can also maintain our psychological wellbeing despite being surrounded by an increasingly stressful world.

Chapter 7 takes on the challenge of looking at how we can maintain the best lifestyle and life balance as possible. Through looking at an amusing theory of life, where life prioritisation and a couple of glasses of wine can help us begin to identify what is really important so that we may then develop a true life balance. This chapter also looks at how we can build a resilience towards the stressors in our work and personal lives.

Chapter 8 looks at whether we need faith either in a higher being or in ourselves. Again tragedy, in terms of the Thai Tsunami, shows the strength of the people gained from having faith in a higher being. A brief history of religious faith and the subsequent growth of humanism and self-belief shows how we seem to be developing more into a society of self-believers rather than religious believers. Having faith in ourselves as well as a pride in our work and our own values seems to be our present God. Then we look to the future of a global internet world without religion and how we can embrace the positive side of this rather than worry about its sinister negative elements. Finally we look at our own faith to leap towards what we truly believe in and what we truly want in life. Having the faith and daring to act may not be enough, however, if we cannot then communicate, to others, who we are or what we want in life.

In **chapter 9** we look at the ways we unconsciously communicate, often in a misleading or incongruent way. Once aware of this we can work towards becoming assertively clear in speaking out towards getting our messages across. Ten simple tips are given for us to get our message across in the most successful way.

Chapter 10, finally concentrates on the tools that will guarantee our success towards daring to live, love and laugh. Important tools for life are given such as overcoming our obstacles, working on our motivation and developing our self-believing, confident behaviour. Listening to our inner voice through co-incidence, intuition or dreams can help us succeed as well as developing the patience and intuition to act. Even being just a little less *'bovvered'* by life can help!! As well as this we are challenged to open up our hearts to love and happiness. Having decided to change our lives, the next challenge is to maintain these changes and not to relapse back into our old habits. We then look at how we can use our growing energy to help others. People like Richard Branson and John Bird have done this through writing about how they achieved their own successes. Finally we look at how Emily Craddock challenged us on the last day of her life – to unite powerfully together to change this imperfect world in order to gain global equality and peace.

1. Moments of Time

Imagine that you are enjoying a flight to your holiday destination, when suddenly, without warning, your jet starts plummeting down to Earth, totally out of control. Passengers are screaming, shouting and crying and there are terrified looks all around. What would you be thinking about during those moments of descent, as you seemingly face certain and immediate death?

This actually happened. A jet came "within seconds of disaster" over Africa, after a passenger stormed into the cockpit and tried to seize the controls. During the struggle the auto-pilot became disengaged and the jumbo plunged thousands of feet through the air. Thankfully, the pilot regained control of the plane just before the point of no return and landed it safely in a nearby airport. As a counseling psychologist and trauma specialist, I helped some of the passengers who had been on the flight. They were suffering from what we call 'Post Traumatic Stress', which includes such reactions as the reliving of the incident through flashbacks or nightmares, feeling emotionally overwhelmed, anxiety, and a sudden exhaustion. The rest of us, who were not there, can never really know how we may have reacted to this near-death situation, but we can imagine what thoughts might have been going through our minds with only seconds to live. For the passengers onboard that flight those seconds seemed like an eternity.

Do any of us really know what is destined for us? None of those passengers could have foreseen that they were to experience such a close shave with death. Similarly, how could those working at the New York World Trade Centre have known that terrorists would fly aeroplanes into their place of work? How could the tourists, enjoying their Christmas break in Thailand, have known that a huge Tsunami would kill hundreds of thousands of people? And likewise, how could the London commuters on the morning of 7th July 2005, have known that suicide bombers were intending to detonate their backpacks full of explosives at various central London destinations? In 2010/11, the earthquakes in Haiti, Chile, New Zealand off the coast of Japan and the floods in Pakistan, Australia and Japan have caused further unexpected deaths and devastation.

Gillian Hicks survived the London bombings but with horrific injuries. She lost both her legs. Despite this, after many months of being in hospital, she walked, with the aid of her new prosthetic legs, onto the stage of the ITV BAFTA award ceremony and made her own personal observation of that fateful day to the audience and TV viewers. She said that, like many others in business, she had been a workaholic but, through nearly dying in this incident, and despite having her legs amputated, she realised that she was just beginning to really appreciate living. She then gently but powerfully reminded the audience to 'Remember to live'. She had realised that many of us forget to do this.

I worked with many of the survivors from most of these events. Whilst awaiting their own possible death through the suffocating tombs of the London underground, they had had to witness many horrific things such as people dying around them, being surrounded by separated limbs, blood and bloodcurdling screams. For those in Tavistock Square, their normal surroundings was turned suddenly into a war zone, with chaos and panic everywhere. They had to wait for nearly an hour for the emergency services to arrive and so set up their own rudimentary first aid posts. Doing the best they could but being left with a huge feeling of guilt that they couldn't do better.

So unprepared are we for sudden death that we are often completely devastated if a tragedy does occur to us or someone close to us. Emily Craddock, to whom this book is dedicated, tragically died at the age of 27. Her mother was so devastated by it that I believe she never really got over it and died of cancer a couple of years later. Her irony was that, as a psychiatrist, she had previously researched the development of terminal illness being linked with extreme grief! If only she could have accepted that we are living in an essentially uncertain and often cruel world.

> *Emily accepted the uncertainty of life when, at age 24, she took a risky job on a Greenpeace activist ship, Arctic Sunrise, as a radio operator and went on many expeditions protesting the abuse of the planet. At six years old she had realised that the barbarous slaughter of seals and whales, along with deforestation for commercial purposes, was wrong so she joined Greenpeace. Three years later, whilst on an anti-logging campaign on the Amazon river, her life was tragically cut short when, inexplicably, she fell from the ship into the river. She, unlike many of us, lived her short life true to her values and beliefs. In fact, on her last day alive she had told an American TV station how much she loved her life and how she had taken constant positive action to carry out what she felt was 'her purpose', right up to the day she died.*

Footnote: In 2009, four of the largest multibillion-dollar companies in the global cattle industry announced their collective agreement to zero deforestation in the Brazilian Amazon. As cattle-ranching is the single largest cause of deforestation in the world, this represents an incredible achievement for Greenpeace, for the forests and for the climate. This change can be attributed to the Greenpeace involvement and perhaps, at least in part, to the increased publicity brought to the anti-deforestation movement by Emily's untimely death.

Many survivors of near-death situations say to me that their experience has had a double effect on their lives. Firstly, gradually getting over the painful physical and psychological effects of the incident in a way makes them realise how strong they really are. Nietzsche, the famous philosopher, said **'What doesn't kill you makes you stronger'.** But more Importantly many have experienced, after an incident, a stark clarity about the fragility of their lives, and the importance of making the most of the life that stretches out in front of them. Some, like Gillian Hicks, had been working far too many hours; some realised that they were living with the wrong person or working at the wrong job; some felt their life had no real meaning or purpose. These, I explained, were common existential thoughts, often experienced after a near-death or traumatic incident, which can catalyse major positive life changes in survivors, leading often to a more authentic and meaningful life. This is what is now termed as *Post Traumatic Growth*. None of us, however, would choose to experience terrifying incidents such as these in order to gain a better life. In fact most of us would probably prefer not to even think about the possibility of untimely death or any death for that matter.

Alan Watts, in his book **Taboo Against Knowing Who You Are,** says 'Animals do not seem to live in constant anxiety about sickness and death, as we do, because they essentially live in the present. But human beings, especially in the West, make death the great bogeyman. He says that this has something to do with the popular Christian belief that the dreaded Last Judgement will follow death, when sinners will be consigned to the temporary horrors of Purgatory or the everlasting agony of Hell. He goes on to say that 'more usual, today, is the fear that death will take us into everlasting nothingness. Imagination cannot grasp nothingness and must therefore fill the void with fantasies of Heaven or just plain denial. Yet death, like birth, is as natural as the leaves falling from the trees in autumn, or the uprooting of a tree following a storm.

Alan Watts looks at life and death as part of a game of 'Black and White' or a game of polar vibrations of existence. He says that if we think about sound, we can realise that it is not continuous but consists of waves of sound and silence. Hearing a melody, we consciously hear only the tones and not the silence. Light, too, is not pure light, but waves of light and darkness but we mostly choose to see the light. Even the universe is a vibration of solid bodies and space yet we consciously look at the planets and the stars and not the space. As in a game there is a fight between the two and one has to win. Sound wins over silence, light wins over darkness and solid bodies win over space. So too, Alan Watts says, does life win over death, which is the so-called battle for survival. He believed that instead of playing the game of 'Black versus White', where one has to win over the other, we should accept each polar vibration equally as part of our existence. To accept the possibility of death as much as we accept the possibility of life. Perhaps, then we could '*Remember to Live*' or '*Say Yes to Life*' as the German philosopher Nietzsche *of the early 20th century* said.

'Dare to become what you are or who you are ....by living to the utmost of our being we are living as we would wish eternally; and the eternal recurrence of time will bring us as near to eternal life as it is possible to get in a world that is finite and bounded.'

Bill Murray, in the film *Groundhog Day*, had his worst day repeated eternally until he did something about it to transform it into his best day ever. Perhaps you are one of the lucky ones, and your answer is '***Yes, my life is just how I want it to be***'. Take a moment of compassion for the rest of us. I shall never forget my beloved grandmother, when I was 11, on her death bed at 89, saying **'*I was never really happy.*'** I resolved, there and then, to determine my own life in such a way that I would never utter such words of regret as I died. This is an extract from a poem by a woman who reviewed her own life at the end of it, aged 80.

> If I had my life to live over, I'd dare to make more mistakes next time. I'd relax, I'd limber up.
>
> I'd be sillier than I have been on this trip. I'd take more chances. I'd take more trips.
>
> I'd climb more mountains and swim more rivers. I'd eat more ice cream and less beans.
> I'd perhaps have more actual troubles but, I'd have fewer imaginary ones.
>
> Oh, I've had my moments and if I had to do it again,
>
> I'd have more moments, I'd try to have nothing else.

How many of us really use freedom of choice to make the best use of our time left?

As we have said the animal kingdom is completely absorbed in its immediate environment, oblivious of past and future, ignorant of its individual freedom. Think of our pets, who are content to just live a pleasant, peaceful and dependent life. Time other than the present is inconceivable to them. Humans, however, do have a sense of time and the freedom to choose how to use it. Yet how many of us really use that freedom to make the best use of our time left?

If we equate a single moment to one second in time, then an average life time of 80 years is made up of just over 2,500 million moments. This may seem a lot, but in one single day you use 86,400 of them. Did you make the best use of yesterday - doing what *you really* wanted to do.

Time is rapidly slipping through our fingers - in reality, tomorrow never comes and the past has gone forever. We may learn from the past and plan for the future, but it also makes sense to be sure we *enjoy* the present. The present moment is inseparable from life.

Eckhart Tolle says, 'Time is where the ego lives on. Almost every thought you think then is concerned with past or future, and your sense of self depends on the past for your identity and on the future for its fulfilment. Fear, anxiety, expectation, regret, guilt, anger are the dysfunctions of the time-bound state of consciousness.

For the ego, the present moment is seen as an obstacle to be overcome. Life, which is now, is seen as a 'problem' and you come to inhabit a world of problems that all need to be solved before you can be happy, fulfilled, or really start living – or so you think. The problem is: For every problem that is solved, another pops up. This is where impatience, frustration, and stress arise, and in our culture, it is many people's everyday reality, their normal state.'

Tolle believes that instead of adding time to oneself, you must remove time. The elimination of time from your consciousness is the elimination of ego. This is not clock time but the elimination of psychological time, 'which is the 'egoic' mind's endless preoccupation with past and future.'

I have seen, within my work, so many people who don't enjoy life for various reasons:

'I don't enjoy my job because it is boring or I work too hard or too many hours', 'I don't enjoy my partner because we are always arguing', 'I don't enjoy my home because it is too noisy', 'I don't enjoy being short of money', 'I don't enjoy being white, black, yellow, man, woman, gay, straight, old, young or ill'.

It is a crazy world we live in, one in which, over the last 100 years, expectations of ourselves and of others have rocketed. Average life expectancy in the developed world has increased from age 60 + to 80 +, and is increasing year on year. At the same time, we seem to be escalating towards excessive stress, alienation, competition and destruction - and for what? Is it for money, for power, for recognition? Or perhaps we are simply striving to live up to others' expectations of us.

These sad stories of not enjoying life continue:

Katherine Ward, *a highly successful, young corporate lawyer, jumped off a London hotel ledge just after Christmas 2005 with much press speculation that she never quite felt that she could live up to neither other people's expectations, nor her own high standards.*

Catherine Bailey, *a top city lawyer, aged 41, threw herself into the Thames in 2009, leaving behind a husband and three young daughters, after struggling to juggle the pressures of work and motherhood as well as meeting the demands she set herself.*

Ricky *jumped in front of a commuter train in 2010 because he had been made redundant and had become so much in debt that he couldn't face his family and friends.*

Caroline, age 34, came to me after her long-term boy-friend suddenly left her. She came originally because she felt suicidal over the break up but then realised she had been living everybody else's life except her own. She just didn't know how to 'Dare to live, love or be happy' any more. Fortunately, she chose to take up the immensely difficult challenge of working with me in order to find a happier and more satisfying existence without the fear of loving again.

How many moments have you used up so far feeling as if you have not really lived or loved or been happy? Perhaps you have had a difficult childhood where you may have suffered criticism, abuse or parents who put their needs above yours. You may have experienced feelings of hurt, anger, despair or loneliness, and the accompanying loss of control? A much more important question, however, is how many moments are you *still* wasting, caught up in past hurts? Perhaps you have become your own critic, your own abuser or your own judge. Perhaps you are still so entangled in past anger, despair and loneliness that you have excluded others?

What about your future? Think about how many 'now' moments we sacrifice for the sake of tomorrow. Putting ourselves on hold until we get older, or when we leave our partner, or when the kids grow up, or when we retire.

How many 'now' moments do you have left before you die (that is if you are really lucky and live until you are 80)? There are about 31.5 million moments in each year you have left. You can start making the most of these moments by reading on and understanding: who you really are; what and who you truly want in life and what makes you most happy?

Freedom and the power of possibility – do you have it?

Perhaps these questions I have put to you are making you feel a little uncomfortable. I hope so, because this is a healthy anxiety that comes from the freedom and power of possibility. Kierkegaard, the 19th century existential philosopher says: *'Anxiety is the possibility of freedom. Once a person realises this they simultaneously understand that they are free.'* He also says that this is what can inspire us to take a 'leap of faith', either towards God, or towards the freedom to really live an authentic life, true to ourselves, before our inevitable death.

In today's modern, free-thinking society, as the power of God and religion is shrinking, like those survivors we can become freer to choose how we want to live. The number of choices is enormous, but with that comes an anxiety which these choices create. Absolute freedom is only achieved when we can freely choose, without feeling anxiety and guilt about what it is that we have chosen. Anxiety and guilt are what makes us run from freedom into the rigidity of rules, which date back from the ancient Ten Commandments to the current laws of the land along with our own value-laden regulations.

The Ten Commandments were created 3000 years ago by 'God', many believe, to help curtail our destructive human urges and to protect us from harm or, perhaps, to protect us from the possibility of too much freedom. For those who cannot remember they are:

One must not:
1. Kill another human being.
2. Steal.
3. Disrespect the Lord.
4. Commit adultery.
5. Tell lies.
6. Worship anything other than God.
7. Disrespect your mother and father.
8. Blame or envy others.
9. Work on Sabbath (God's day).
10. Make any statues of other gods or bow to them

But how appropriate are these rather restrictive rules, with their emphasis on the negative, to our modern world? Today, flouting of the Ten Commandments has become habitual for most of us in our everyday lives. How many of us are guilty of 'borrowing' something when we know we cannot or will not give it back; guilty of avoiding taxes; guilty of blaming or envying others, lying, or disrespecting our parents or others? Many of us have bowed to other gods such as the political gods, the fashion gods, the multi-media gods, the popular culture gods or even the social expectation gods. As for working on God's day, that long ago became the norm.

Modern science and technology enables us to live longer, be more comfortable, have more choices and live more complex lives. But have we really become freer and happier or are we, instead, becoming more stressed, anxious and depressed?

Author, George Cockcroft, illustrates this dilemma through his novel *The Dice Man*. The narrator, a psychiatrist, Luke Rhinehart, a husband and a father, is locked down by routine and order, experiencing extreme existential angst and despair. The narrator attempts to then do something about it through turning to chance by picking up the dice and living his life through chance. This is a quote from his book.

'My colleagues, and even myself, all asserted that my problem was absolutely normal: I hated myself and the world because I had failed to face and accept the limitations of myself and of life. In literature this refusal is called romanticism; in psychology, neurosis. The assumption is that a limited and bored self is the unavoidable, all-embracing norm. And I was beginning to agree until, after a few months of wallowing in depression (I had furtively purchased a .38 revolver and nine cartridges), I came washing up on the shore of Zen.........The world of the rat race, which I had assumed to be normal and healthy for an ambitious young man, seemed suddenly like the world of a rat race. I was stunned and converted. Seeing drive, greed and intellectual aspiration as meaningless and sick in my colleagues, I was able to make the unusual generalization to myself; I too had the same symptoms of grasping after illusions. The secret, I seemed to learn, was in not caring, in accepting limitations, conflicts and ambiguities of life with joy and satisfaction, in effortless drifting with the flow of impulse. So life was meaningless: Who cares? So my ambitions are trivial? Pursue them anyway. Life seems boring. Yawn. I followed impulse. I drifted. I didn't care. Unfortunately life seemed to get more boring. Admittedly I was cheerfully, even gaily bored, where before I had been depressingly bored, but life remained essentially uninteresting. My mood of happy boredom was theoretically preferable to my desire to rape and kill, but personally speaking not much. It was about this stage of my somewhat sordid road to truth that I discovered the Dice'. 'Easy: let the dice decide and roll with it. Then you will not be responsible. It will be fate!! The dice don't do rules; the dice do life.'

With his every act determined by a throw of the dice, the narrator set out to overthrow the tyranny of his own personality. He had a vision of a new man — a random man, unfettered by the normal human limitations of habit, routine and the law. In this lunatic quest, he lurched from one outrage to the next. From respectable but bored beginnings as a successful psychiatrist and happily married father, through uninhibited sexual experimentation and flirtations with madness and murder, he ends up a fugitive, a hunted enemy of the state.

Whereas the above excerpt was amusing fiction, the reality stands today that, whilst we are surrounded by amazing technology and knowledge, we are also increasingly surrounded by strangers, material possessions, stress and general unhappiness. Without having to go to such extremes, however as the Dice Man or a near death survivor, we can choose to awaken up to life, to '*Dare to have...... Lived, Loved, Laughed*'.

I even dare to suggest that the groups of Ten Tips I give in my chapters might be more appropriate than the Ten Commandments in that they help both to curtail our negative human drives but also to encourage our positive human drives.

In doing so we can ask ourselves such questions as 'Who and what is important to me?';
'Do I feel completely happy and fulfilled?';
'What is my purpose and meaning in life' and even 'Who am I?

What is your purpose in life?
Robin Sharma quotes from *The Monk who sold his Ferrari:*

When you are inspired by some great purpose, some extraordinary project, all your thoughts break their bonds; your mind transcends limitations, your consciousness expands every direction and you find yourself in a new, great and wonderful world. Dormant forces, faculties and talents become alive and you discover yourself to be a greater person than you ever dreamed yourself to be. The boundaries of your life are merely creations of the self. If you want to live a more peaceful, meaningful life, you must think more peaceful, meaningful thoughts.'

According to the Dalai Lama, exiled Tibetan Buddhist and author of many books on life, love and happiness, the questions *"What haven't I got?"* and *"What is missing from my life?"* can lead a person into a life of insatiable craving, envy and chronic dissatisfaction. Conversely, the question **"Why am I here?",** he says, can challenge a person to seek deeper ways of defining themselves.

"We find ourselves moving from craving to meaning as a basis to living, and with that shift, we find an enormous wellspring of energy and motivation. Once we derive our motivation from something that continuously refuels our connection to others and our soul, it's like a circle that just keeps replenishing itself. We've tapped into an infinite life force that breeds happiness in a way no possession ever could."

Most of us, sadly, are simply too busy to take time to ask ourselves why we're living the way we are. 'Why am I here?' challenges us to look deeper within ourselves - to find our purpose in life.

Why are you here? What is your purpose in life?

How sure are you that this will happen? 1 = impossible; 10 = certain.

1   2   3   4   5   6   7   8   9   10

If you are finding it difficult to identify your purpose, then it may help to first to think about what is really important to you now, both personally and at work? These represent your core values.

What is important to you in life?
(Tick those relevant to you)

Exercise 1
What are your core Values in your Personal Life?

Prosperity	Personal growth
Having an intimate loving relationship	Standing up for my beliefs
Helping others	Making time for friendships
Self-reliance	
Having stimulating experiences	Stability and order
Enjoying a leisurely life	Honesty
Sincerity	Physical health
Open-mindedness	Reliability
Taking care of loved ones	Creativity
	Spiritual meaning

What are your core Values in your Personal Life?

Self-respect	Manners
Loyalty	Being cheerful
Tidiness	Independence
Being respected by others	Freedom of choice

What are your core Values in your Work Life?

Making the best use of my abilities	Ambition and advancement
Being practical	Being part of a team
Trying out my own methods	Being secure
Being "somebody"	Having power and authority
Accomplishment	Controlling others
Variety	Communicating to others
Being highly paid	Creating things or being artistic
Using my own judgement	Teaching people
Working autonomously	Decision making
Being busy	Being able to use modern technology
Integrity	Listening to others
Telling people what to do	Driving a vehicle
Receiving praise	
Helping other people	

Now write down **your top 5 core** values across your personal and work life.

1.

2.

3.

4.
5.

It may be interesting to see if most of these core values have come from your personal or work life. Do your current commitments allow you the time you want to devote to these core values?

Now create a vision of your purpose

Having identified what really is important to you, now is a good time to create a vision that supports your values and your purpose. This wonderfully relaxing meditation will help you to create that vision.

Exercise 2

Lie flat on your back with eyes closed, shoes off and undo anything that is tight. Start to relax your body and mind completely. Breathe in deeply and count to 5 then breathe out and count to 5 and follow this pattern throughout the exercise. Now start with your feet and tense the muscles in your toes and lower legs. Hold the tension for a few seconds, then relax. Feel the difference between tension and relaxation. Then do the same thing in turn, with your thighs, your stomach, your arms and your face. Tense then relax. As you are doing this clear your mind and focus on your whole body relaxing quite heavily into the floor. Let go of all the tension and listen to the sound of your calm, even breathing – very gentle and very shallow. You may begin to feel as if you are floating. Let it happen and let go of reality and think about would make up your ideal life.

- *Where would you like to be, ideally?*
- *How would you like to look?*
- *What would you ideally like to be doing, either at work or at home?*
- *Who would you ideally want to be with?*

Lie still for a few moments and think about where you have taken yourself – and when you feel ready begin to get up slowly and write down your experience and then answer these questions

Where would you like to be living? *Is this a big city or a town or village?*

What would you like to be doing?
- *At work:*
- *At home:*

How would you like your financial situation to be?

Who would you like to be with you?
- *Relationship*
- *Family*
- *Friends*

How you would like to feel/look?
- *In your body*
- *In your mind*

Were you surprised by what has come out of this exercise? Many people are, because this exercise often cuts through our conscious thinking and touches our subconscious. Hold on to this vision whilst you explore more of your self. You can draw and colour these images if you want. Did your vision fit the purpose you wrote down initially? If not, then re-write it below.

Why are you here? What is your purpose in life?

How sure are you that this will happen? 1 = impossible; 10 = certain.

1   2   3   4   5   6   7   8   9   10

Now think about how you can change things in your life to fit in with your vision and set some goals accordingly.

Also remember the words of *Robin Sharma from The Monk Who Sold His Ferrari*

Once you figure out your passion/destiny and take the risk of moving out of your comfort zone, your work will become play. Saying that you don't have time to improve your thoughts and your life is like saying you don't have time to stop for petrol because you are too busy driving. Or time to eat healthily. Eventually you and your car will lose their power and stop.'

If you want to have the inner strength to achieve a goal you need discipline eg. To get up earlier or go to the gym or to meditate or to eat less and more healthily – envision yourself as lean, fit, attractive and healthy, with boundless energy and vitality. If you want to read more, worry less, be more patient or be more loving - all you have to do is control your thoughts. When you control your mind, then you control your life. And once you control your life you become the master of your destiny.'

The following chapters will help you with this.

2. Dare to Live

'***Dare to become who your are or what you are***' says the philosopher Nietzsche. Those who care for us most, often say, as we leave them, 'Take care' rather than 'Dare to be who you are'. Perhaps they fear that if we take a risk then something terrible might happen. But are those caring words also stopping us from the freedom that comes from daring? That fear of daring can become so internalised that we can then stop ourselves from taking risks of extending our lives.

'If I leave my job I may not get another one that's as good'; *'If I leave my partner I might not be able to cope on my own'; 'If I stand up in public I might make a huge fool of myself'.*

As we have seen severe crises, particularly those that endanger lives, often open the door to the freedom of possibility of 'Daring to Live, Love and be Happy'. Recognising death as a very real possibility, we have seen that survivors often begin to wonder whether they are living their lives in the way that they truly want to. However, in the aftermath, usually because of the anxiety that accompanies such freedom of possibility, people often then choose to close that door tightly shut again. This is when they make excuses for not Daring to Live, such as: *"I have to pay the mortgage so I can't leave my job"* or *"I don't want to leave my partner until the kids grow up"* or *"I can't stand up in public because I am too nervous."*

What is your reason for not daring to live?

John Bird, self-made man and founder of The Big Issue, says in his book *How to Change your Life in 7 Steps*:

> 'Anybody can make the best of the best times in life, but the real trick is to make the best of the worst times. If you look at successful people in life, you may find something really interesting – that a lot of them make their own breaks and usually when they are failing. They never thought about being victims, instead they saw this time of difficulty as an opportunity to reinvent their lives.'
> John Bird How to Change your Life in 7 Steps

In fact these successful people have *'Dared to Live'* in order to get to where they wanted to be. **How often do you take risks without worrying about getting it wrong?** Many of my clients have said that they daren't do anything because of a huge fear of failure. Some even prefer to die than to fail, as may have been the case with the two city lawyers Katherine Ward and Catherine Bailey. A client of mine, Sharon, had forgotten the joys of daring:

> **Sharon** *came to me in despair. She had lost her beloved cat, had just been made redundant from her long-term job and her husband, Richard, whom she had been with for nearly 20 years, had told her he wanted to split. She was finding it very difficult to come to terms with being alone again after such a long time, and felt very upset and angry about the split with Richard. She interpreted her relationship as being the thing that was most important to her in life. By recognising this as being her main priority, she then realised that both her and Richard, along the way, had let go of their earlier values. When they both met at a Kibbutz, they shared strong environmental and altruistic ideals and both were vegetarians. This compatibility had been part of the bedrock of their relationship. Somehow they had both then fallen into mundane jobs, which neither particularly enjoyed, had taken on a big mortgage and bought a cat as a substitute for a child. Although Sharon was still devastated at the loss of her relationship with Richard, she gradually began to focus on her previous passions, particularly her desire to help people and the environment. Around the same time as Sharon's personal crisis, the Tsunami had devastated parts of Thailand, India, Sri Lanka, Indonesia and The Maldives. Although she felt extremely anxious about her new life alone, Sharon realised that she wanted to take the risk of going to Thailand to help the survivors there.*

When I saw her a year later she told me how she had been part of a voluntary project working to rebuild homes and lives for the people of Thailand, and how much fun she had had working with the Thai people and other like-minded volunteers. By taking the risk of returning to her true passions, she said she had felt more alive and happier than ever before.

Caroline, the client I have already mentioned also felt that she wanted to change her life after nearly ending it. She had realised how unhappy she was, dwelling on her past. She had developed a highly compliant personality from an early age, going to the school her parents had chosen and studying subjects she hated in order to please them. She had then attained a first class degree after working extremely hard at Oxford – so hard, in fact, that she had come close to a nervous breakdown. She got a job at a top management consultancy and became one of their most prized consultants. But, throughout all this, she felt neither happy, nor good enough. She was totally exhausted by working long hours and rarely took time for a holiday. The more she talked about her childhood, the more she realised that, as far back as she could remember, she had been seeking her parents' approval. She felt that unless she constantly pleased them, they would reject her. She had found out, years before, that she had been an unplanned baby, and realised she had always been desperately seeking to gain a 'legitimate' place in her own family, primarily through extreme compliance. Her core purpose seemed solely to please others.

Both Sharon and Caroline dared to work with me towards changing their lives. For Sharon her changes gave her, almost immediately, a more enjoyable life-style; for Caroline it took longer but eventually life began to seem less daunting for her.

Are you a Daring personality?

Daring personalities have often proved to be successful personalities. A propensity to be daring is usually accompanied by the complementary qualities of optimism, decisiveness and resilience. Many successful leaders in business, politics and sport let criticism roll off their backs, make decisions easily, have confidence, sleep better and breeze through the day with energy to spare.

When Roger Bannister, in 1954, first hit that seemingly impossible target of running a four-minute mile, three other people did the same within the following 12 months. He not only broke a time barrier, but also a psychological barrier, thus encouraging other athletes to believe that they could do the same. We have seen footballers, when they are at the top of their game, or 'in the zone', seem relaxed and confident under pressure. David Beckham, who at his peak had high self-belief and little fear of failure, so when he took crucial penalty kicks he could effectively apply all his skills and get the ball in the net.

Top tennis player Roger Federer, who had won six consecutive Wimbledon titles, put his mental toughness and success down to his positive attitude and ability to keep negative emotions out of his game. He stays focused on what he wants. He wants to win, he can feel how it would be to win and not be afraid of losing. With those feelings and thoughts he generates a lot of positive energy. The only thoughts in his mind are about winning, the trophy and how he will feel when that happens. That is his most special mental ability – that he can enter 'the zone' almost on command. He is the master of the inner game, where he plays instinctively, courageously and creatively. Perhaps his sudden defeat in 2010 was due to the distraction of his new twins!!

Tiger Woods, in 2008, was unbeaten for over seven months in seven tournaments – a winning streak not seen in golf for more than a half-century. He puts that success down to not being burdened by self-defeating thoughts, nor an obsession with results, so that he can focus exclusively on the task in hand. Like others he had entered 'the zone'. Tiger, like Roger Federer, loves to compete: he loves to win and hates to lose, but is able to gain the biggest rush from the battle itself, and release his attachment to the outcome. Unfortunately, allegedly, he too succumbed to a number of distractions, which led to him compromising his game.

Other sports and business people can be self-limiting in their views about their ability and capacity to succeed. They have a mindset that says, 'I can't do that'. These people often find that fear of failure, or other negative emotions, can affect their normally refined skills. This was defined by the sports psychologist, Dr Willi Raillo, as 'choking' behaviour, which can lead to the very failure that is feared. Even Beckham got sent off in the 1998 World Cup when he lost his temper!

In order perhaps to answer the question – are you a daring personality, perhaps we should first approach that age-old, elusive quandary – 'Who am I to be daring?' If you don't really know who you are or do not accept yourself, then how can you move beyond yourself. Some parts of our selves have the ability to be daring whilst others can draw us back into safety.

Our Many Selves

By the time a person reaches adulthood, they have developed many different 'selves'. This does not mean, however, that we all have multiple personality disorders. Some of those selves we may be proud of and love about ourselves, whilst other parts of ourselves we may not be so proud of, or even hate.

Caroline, I discovered, had many different selves. The ones she liked were her nurturing self, her childlike self, her sexy self, her performer self, her intellectual self and her career-focused self. The ones she didn't like and often preferred to deny were her rather manipulative, cunning self or her extremely self-critical self, or her perfectionist self. Despite being a successful career woman, there was a child within her screaming to break free from all her responsibilities and just play; the sexy self fantasised about a Sunday spent with her attentive lover; her reflective, intellectual self yearned for a discussion with like-minded people, or to read the Sunday papers or a stimulating book; her career self wanted to focus more intently on her career ambitions; and her performer self simply wanted to perform, either to her friends telling her best joke or to an audience talking intellectually about her work. Then her critical self told her that she was worthless and ugly so she would have a few drinks in order to try to expel these thoughts. But that, more often than not, simply fuelled her self-loathing to the extent that she would eventually self-harm, usually by cutting herself.

Exercise 3 – our many selves

What about your selves? Put a tick by your selves you like and cross for you selves you don't like.

Performing( ), daring( ), resilient( ), sensitive( ), kind( ), sympathetic( ), physical( ), intellectual( ), assertive ( ), punctual ( ), proactive( ), reliable( ), stable ( ), disciplined( ), honest ( ), skilled ( ), qualified( ), motivated( ), adaptable ( ), organised( ), determined ( ), nurturing( ), caring( ), sexual( ), childish( ), responsible( ), creative( ), leader( ), practical( ), analytical( ), mature( ), empathic( ), witty( ), funny( ), friendly( ), artistic( ), serious( ), problem solver( ), communicator( ), judge( ), detective( ),

peacemaker( ) shy( ), passive( ), cautious( ), neurotic( ),
worrier( ), manic( ), hurrier( ), chaotic( ), angry( ), ag-
gressive( ) perfectionist( ), pleaser( ), tryer( ), strong( )
controller( ), loner( ), guilty( ), depressed( ), careless ( ).

Our influences

I mentioned that our different selves have developed
gradually from childhood. From that time we have been
influenced by many people including family, teachers,
mentors, friends, role models, books, films, places or
even strangers. These could be positive influences in
terms of praise, love and positive nurturing; or negative
influences in terms of criticism, hatred, envy cr abuse.

*Caroline, our high flyer, took a long time to build her self-esteem
and shake off her extremely negative influences – a mother who
constantly found everything wrong with her and criticised her,
a grandmother who was hateful towards her and an abusive
family friend. More importantly she began to accept that she
was not, and could never be, perfect and that there were parts of
herself that she was not particularly proud of. She did gradually
tackle these aspects of her personality, as well as realising that
she did not have to almost kill herself in an effort to please others
and that many people liked her 'just the way she was'. She now
is maybe at an 80% level of self-love and acceptance, which may
be as much as she can hope for, but she is a great deal happier*

than ever before. By realizing that she need not be perfect, she also realized that it was OK for others to be imperfect. This has made her feel more satisfied in her relationships with men as she does not demand perfection from them.

Like Caroline what is important is for us to realise that, as an adult, we can choose our influences and reject those who try to influence us negatively. Also we can choose to adopt the self that we love whilst working on reducing those parts of ourselves that we do not feel so comfortable with.

Exercise 4 – your influences

Family Influences

Praised for:
Criticised for:
I loved my family life because
I hated my family life because

Influences from teachers, friends, mentors or other

Praised for:
Criticised for:
I loved school because:
I hated school because:

Who I admire and why:
Favourite books, films, places, people:

Obstacles to Daring

Just as we are ready to dare then don't we so often find that there are obstacles that get in our way.

Guilt as an Obstacle to Daring

We often assume guilty people are those who have broken the law, yet most inmates I have met, within my work, profess to be innocent, whilst the truly innocent spend their lives wracked with guilt.

> *Helen continuously walked around with her head hung low. It didn't matter what she did or didn't do, she felt guilty. She talked at length about her guilt, but couldn't seem to do anything to get rid of it and most of her energy was taken up with what I call 'inappropriate guilt'. She constantly thought about what she 'could', 'should' or 'ought' to have done. Doing things that other people wanted her to do helped her feel less guilty about her own selfish feelings and needs. I helped her to decipher what was appropriate for her to feel guilty about, and what was not. I explained that if she had murdered her boss then perhaps her guilt might have been appropriate but just by wanting him to disappear is not worthy of feeling guilty! Also being what I call 'healthily selfish' is not something that one should feel guilty about.*

Many people feel inappropriate guilt for loved ones they have lost. Survivor guilt' is generally inappropriate and can be quite crippling. I have talked to many survivors of tragic incidents who have felt terribly guilty by the fact that they survived when their friends, family, colleagues, or even strangers have died instead. They often think 'If only I had done more for them' or 'If only I hadn't let them do that' or 'If only I had been there to help'. We can only do the best we can, based on the knowledge we had at the time. '

Sally, *a young survivor of a Middle Eastern pleasure boat tragedy, lost her husband when he was trapped in the lower deck as the boat capsized. On that tragic evening she suddenly felt, that she needed to go to the upper deck, and urged her husband to go with her. He, however, had not felt the same urgency and wanted to finish his conversation with a colleague. She was the last person to escape from the lower deck before the boat started to capsize, sending water rushing down the stairs and blocking the exit. Sally felt enormous guilt that she had 'left him behind to die', through saving herself. She had even, whilst in the water, seen her trapped husband through the boat window and had beckoned him to come over to it while she hopelessly tried to break the glass for him to escape. But plexi-glass boat windows are almost impossible to break, and she saw him mouth the words 'I love you' to her as the water consumed him. She was, in those first few days, in total shock and overwhelmed by grief and guilt*

James had meant to catch the Paddington to Cardiff train on the day it crashed, but he had jumped out to grab a coffee and missed it. He was devastated that he had not been there to help his friends whom he normally travelled with from and to Reading each day. He thought that if he had been there he could have perhaps saved some of their lives.

Overcoming guilt

Guilt may sometimes be appropriate, in that you actually did do something that hurt another person, broke the law or betrayed your own values. If this is the case, then you can often do something that can help repair what you did. If, however, you decide that your guilt is inappropriate then just dismiss it as such.

What things do you feel guilty about and how might you overcome this?

Anxiety as an Obstacle to Daring

As we have seen in the case of some sportsmen, excessive emotion, anxiety or distractions can seriously undermine the ability to accomplish goals. Although it is healthy to be concerned about things, anxiety caused by excessive worrying is debilitating. Anxiety is produced in us when there are threats to our self-esteem through the embarrassment of possible failure. If, therefore, we are asked to do something like giving a speech, we may worry about doing it badly and thus be shown up as a fool. Physical symptoms of anxiety include muscle tension, sweaty palms, an upset stomach, shortness of breath and a pounding heart. When we remain in a constant state of anxiety, in the absence of a definite solution, then it can turn into panic.

***Patsy** felt that her constant anxiety about life's challenges was stopping her from living. She worried about her husband; she worried about her children, despite them being fully-grown; she worried about the weather and about global warming and terrorism. In fact she worried about almost everything. She rarely missed seeing the news or reading the newspaper, so that she might seek confirmation of her anxieties. She constantly told people to be careful rather than enjoy life. I asked her whether either of her parents had been anxious and she told me that her older brother had died as an infant and as a result her mother had 'wrapped her up in cotton wool' throughout her childhood. She then realised that she had been trying to do the same thing with her own family, but that in doing so was also preventing them - as well as herself - from truly living. The only time that she could recall ever having taken a risk was in learning to drive. Such was her anxiety regarding this that it took her nine attempts before she passed her test. Once she passed she threw away her licence and never drove again as she said she felt more comfortable being 'driven' by others. I commented that this may have also become a metaphor for her approach to life in general, and she agreed and wept about this. Even though she was nearly 60, she dearly wanted to be able to take more risks and to feel safe doing so.*

We looked at various ways for her to take small risks each day. By doing this she gently began to learn that the world was not going to end if she took the odd risk, and she never looked back. In fact, she told me it was as if her life had started from that point.

Fear as an Obstacle to Daring

We have many fears that challenge us. These can be divided up into situation based fears, ego based fears and choking fears. Tick those you may identify with.

Exercise 5 – your fears
Situation based fears

Those out of our control	Those we face as choices
becoming disabled	breaking the law
compulsory retirement	changing career
being alone	making friends
child leaving home	end or start of relationship
change	making a presentation
loss of money	gain or loss of weight
dying	asserting oneself
war	driving
illness	being interviewed
accidents	making a mistake
being a victim of crime	intimacy

Ego based fears

Those out of our control	Those we face as choices
Rejection	being conned
Success	helplessness
Failure	disapproval
being vulnerable	loss of face

Choking fears

If we convince ourselves we can't do something then we are likely to experience choking behaviour, which may prevent us from doing that very thing.

Overcoming anxiety and fear

Anxiety and fear can be reduced through adopting various strategies:

Putting issues into perspective - Whatever you're worrying about, look at it in terms of how much it will affect your life or the world in a month, in a year or in five years time. Looking at the preoccupations of your own life 'in the grand scheme of things' was a phrase first coined by the philosopher, Spinoza, in the 17th Century.

Being honest with yourself - Be honest with yourself and accept whatever you don't know and sincerely communicate what you do know.

Prepare and practise - By preparing, practising, visualising as well as accepting the concept of failure as part of taking a risk, then, anxiety can be reduced considerably.

Self-Esteem as the Key to Reducing Obstacles to Daring

Self-esteem is the combination of self-confidence, self-acceptance and self-belief. People with high self-esteem are able to solve problems rather than worry about them, can confront or eliminate things that frighten them, can take calculated risks and know how to nurture and reward themselves. Many of my clients arrive at my consulting room with very low self-esteem. Usually they have grown up with criticism rather than praise, or have suffered some form of abuse that has made them feel worthless, helpless or 'bad'.

Hayley came to me in a suicidal state, saying that she was completely alone in the world and that she hated herself so much that she felt the world would be a better place without her. She presented herself as utterly worthless and very depressed. Through talking to me it turned out that her mother had never liked her. She was never praised for her achievements. Instead she was criticised for even the smallest things. She was considered to be a 'bad 'un' from the time she was born, whereas her older brother could do no wrong. We spent a long time looking at her achievements. Instead of Hayley reaffirming each day that she was somehow 'bad' or useless, she practised affirmations that stated how good she was at so many things. Instead of believing that she was not worth being loved by others she gradually was able to love herself more, and in doing so she could allow others in to love her.

It is rarely possible, however, to just switch on self-esteem, but by working at it and by thinking positively about what we can do best, we can build our confidence and so reduce our anxiety, fear and guilt.

Self-Confidence

Self-confidence is the conviction that we are competent enough to cope with life's changes and challenges. A healthy sense of self-confidence is a critical factor in overcoming fear. Low self-confidence inhibits our efforts to move ahead, to meet challenges, and to take risks in pursuit of our objectives. Inflated self-confidence can equally be hazardous. Those who suffer from this are continually subject to frustration, disappointment and rage when reality doesn't validate their idealized view of themselves. Their arrogance also often distances them from others

Self Acceptance

Self acceptance is gained by embracing and being proud of those parts of ourselves that we do love. Then looking at the parts of ourselves that we're not so proud of and either accepting them doing something about them.

Self Belief

Self-belief is the impression that we are worthy of success and happiness. Fiona Harrold, one of UK's leading life coaches, is probably the country's greatest self-believer. She says:

'Self-belief is your greatest ally. You've just got to be able to turn it on and boost it when you need it most. It's part of the armoury of all people who achieve great things. To win at anything in your life, your greatest battle is with yourself. The person who has the weapon to make you win or lose is you. Your weapon is your mind. Your mental approach makes you strong or weak, tough or flabby. Conquering yourself is the ultimate challenge. Great self-believers have the edge. They carry within them a formidable advantage over the average person. They know how to dig deep and muster additional resources and back-off when necessary. They never lose. They always live to fight another day.' Fiona Harrold

I went to see Fiona when I was going through a period of low self-belief. She helped me believe in myself again enough to begin writing this book.

Increasing Self-Esteem

As we have seen with many sports and business people, having high self-esteem gives them the confidence and self-belief to be able to dare to fail. They have learnt, through their failures and have been proud of their successes.

Positive feedback

Think about the people you know who are always giving you genuine compliments, encouragement and warm hugs. These are what I call positive strokes. My dear friend and mentor, Jenny, constantly gave me genuine compliments, praise and sincere warmth and hugs for many years. Initially I found it really difficult to accept them and shrugged them off, but gradually she showed me the value of accepting them by smiling and saying 'Thank you'. From her I also learned how to similarly give positive feedback to others, including, most importantly, my own family and myself. Despite her terminal cancer, at too young an age, she stayed positive and still had the energy to give out her warmth and compliments right up to the day of her death. Now I hear her voice within me still giving out those compliments!

Positive strokes can be mental, such as praise, thanks, or a nod of approval. It can be a warm cuddle, or a kind deed. It has been proven that it is these positive affirmations and experiences that make us feel calm, relaxed and happy, whilst constant negative comments and experiences make us feel fed up, angry, frustrated, and stressed.

Positive self-talk

Talking yourself up is a sure way of increasing your self-esteem. This, however, is easier said than done and needs daily practice.

Exercise 6 – positive self talk

Reminding yourself about your achievements and what
you like about yourself can be a good start.

1. What was my greatest achievement?
2. I have helped others by……..
3. What do I value about me?
4. What do I like about me?
5. What is the most interesting thing about me?
6. What is the best decision I ever made?
7. If I really want I can….
8. The most difficult thing I ever did………….

Repeating daily positive affirmations

- I accept, love and approve of myself and am
  uniquely me
- I can look and feel great
- I deserve to be happy and fulfilled both at home and
  at work
- I am doing the best I can and will be less hard
  on myself

Overcoming negative feedback

Think about how you feel after someone has given
you negative feedback. Perhaps they have criticised
you or put you down in some way. Usually this makes
us feel quite hurt or angry. If their criticism, however, is appropriate we may then choose to change our
behaviour, but too much criticism or inappropriate

criticism just lowers our self esteem. Perhaps it would be better to think of ourselves as an umbrella in the rain and let all criticisms, unless really valid and constructive, just bounce straight off us.

Some quick reminders for increasing your self-esteem.

1. Dare to live and take risks
2. Welcome positive feedback and avoid negative feedback unless valid
3. Be kind to yourself as well as to others
4. Take care of your health and appearance
5. Keep a journal of your achievements and reward yourself for them
6. Learn from your and others failures.
7. Be lighter and laugh with others

3. Dare to Love

Love is a word that we, perhaps, put far too much trust in, without even realising what exactly it is. Yet, as Oscar Wilde put it, '***Who, being loved, is poor?***' Humans need to be nourished by love as much as they need to be nourished by food and water. There are many different types of love, which take us on journeys towards happiness and sadly also towards despair. Surviving the worst crises can, however, re-enforce our need for love. One of the worst cases of my crisis work was with Camu.

__Camu__ was a young 32 year old single professional woman, who had been drug raped at a party when she was only 17. Three drunk men had drugged her and taken her away from the party to abuse her at their leisure. Survivors of most tragedies at least survive and suffer accompanied by other victims and thus create loving bonds between them, unlike Camu, who suffered alone for many years until she had the courage to talk about it.

Studies have shown that people within communities feel a greater sense of support, contentment and happiness than those who are isolated. Despite this, an increasing number of people find themselves alone and unsupported by either a community or a loving intimate relationship. Quite often they fill this gap with 'material' attachment such as cars, fashionable clothes or other status symbols or even with the accruement of power.

Through the internet, people pursue 'virtual intimacy' within 'chat' rooms, 'dating' websites and now even with avatars. That 'virtual intimacy' extends through to movies, television and sport, which have introduced 'love' icons such as Marilyn Munro, Tom Cruise, Johnny Depp, Michael Buble and now teenybopper Justin Bieber!! Sports icons include footballer, David Beckham and tennis player Rafael Nadal. All serve to create a fantasy, which then feeds into a love mania. Alternatively gripping soap opera storylines, whilst comfort eating or drinking can be addictive as a way of averting isolation. All of these habits are poor substitutes, however, for good old-fashioned human intimacy, which comes free, only from genuine relationships.

Genuine relationships are REAL and based on the true human emotions of trust, closeness, love and affection, through which one gains a sense of sharing and connectedness. Genuine relationships are based on a willingness, firstly to open up to one particular person romantically, or to family, friends or even strangers, then to gradually form genuine, deep and trusting bonds, based on common humanity: shared physical space, feelings, thoughts and ideas. But to open up to a genuine or REAL relationship one must also be prepared to be HURT. I read a wonderful little children's book called the 'Velveteen Rabbit', where a rabbit was sad and lonely in the toy cupboard because he had never been loved. He asked the skin horse what is REAL and how could he become REAL. The skin horse told the rabbit that he could only become REAL when he was truly loved by someone. And the rabbit said 'Does it hurt?' Sometimes said the horse but when you are REAL you don't mind being hurt occasionally.

REAL love and connection has to be constantly renewed and revitalised, otherwise the intimacy can wane. And that involves supreme effort! Within genuine relationships each partner supports and nurtures the other's individual and shared growth. We must, therefore, be able to see our partners, friends, children or family as separate human individuals, with their own strengths, weaknesses and needs and their own pathway to growth. Kahil Gibran puts this well in his poem:

On Children

Your children are not your children.

They are the sons and daughters of Life's longing for itself.

They come through you but not from you,

And though they are with you yet they belong not to you.

You may give them your love but not your thoughts,

For they have their own thoughts.

You may house their bodies but not their souls,

For their souls dwell in the house of tomorrow,

which you cannot visit, not even in your dreams.

You may strive to be like them,

but seek not to make them like you.

For life goes not backward nor tarries with yesterday

Many couples forget these important points and instead develop painful and damaging relationships. Jan and Ed are a couple who came to see me as a last resort as they were on the point of breaking up over their differences about what they believed was a genuine relationship.

Jan and Ed had been married for 20 years and had raised three children. Both of their own childhoods had been spent within busy families where the motto was 'children should be seen and not heard'. Ed had been sent to a childminder for most of his young childhood, as both his parents worked hard at their full *time jobs. Jan had been part of a chaotic family struggling to make ends meet. Both Jan and Ed felt that their needs, as children, seemed to be less important than those of their family as a whole. When they had children of their own, Jan wanted to put her children's needs first, so she gave up her career ambitions in order to be a more present and attentive mother. She decided to work in a less involved, part time job. Ed, however, still believed that children's needs should come second to those demanded by his work. He wanted to make his business as successful as he could, in order to be the principal provider as well as the head of the household, just as his own father had always been. There began the divide. Life was frustrating and stressful for them both, trying to balance their working lives with family life, and each competed for time off. Then, just as their lives were getting easier and the children were becoming more independent, both Jan's and Ed's parents, now elderly, needed more care, which took up what little time they had left. The problem was that in all this caring for others, Ed and Jan had forgotten how to care for themselves and, worse, they had forgotten how to care for each other, which put a considerable strain on their relationship.*

Adam Philips says: 'The most difficult task for every couple is to get the right amount of misunderstanding'

Jan and Ed had so much misunderstanding between them it was severely affecting the level of happiness in their relationship. Each thought that the other did not care. Each thought the other selfish, and there was a constant power struggle for time and position. The psychologist and author Philips also says:

'Too little (understanding) and you assume you know each other. Too much, and you begin to believe there must be someone else, somewhere, who does understand you. We have affairs when we get our proportions wrong.'

Jan grew increasingly jealous of Ed's space away from the family, suspecting that he might be having an affair. What Jan hadn't realised was that Ed was also jealous of the time Jan spent with her work colleagues, whom she seemed to admire and respect so much. Ed never felt admired in the same way by Jan so he eventually did have an affair with someone who admired him.

Jealousy is such a powerful negative emotion. Abraham Maslow, an American psychologist says:

'It (jealousy) is never, then, a function of love but of our insecurities and dependencies. It is the fear of a loss of love and it destroys that very love.'

Jan had become so insecure in her relationship with Ed, she had, in fact, helped to push him away from her into a real affair. As her suspicions grew stronger that Ed was being unfaithful to her, Jan lost trust and checked his mobile to find intimate messages from one of her own girlfriends. She told me that on viewing this she suddenly felt sick, with an immense heaviness in her abdomen and waves of rage sweeping over her from this deep betrayal of trust.

'Trust is a word we have put too much trust in' **Adam Philips.**

I believe that most of us put far too much importance on the word 'trust'. How often have we heard the words **"I trusted him/her with my life and he/she betrayed me so now he/she is not worth knowing".** Only those who have experienced a deep betrayal of trust can know the intense pain it causes. People have likened it to the initial stages of grief, with shock and disbelief followed by feelings of abandonment. So why do we react so deeply to the betrayal of trust? Perhaps our experience of trust begins with the first perfect relationship we had with our parents, when as infants we trusted them to keep us alive. In our adult relationships, however, as with Jan and Ed, life and baggage gets in the way of that trust and mistakes are made.

Although Ed immediately gave up his affair and they had couple's counselling, it only served to paper over the cracks of much deeper issues. Jan could not 'forgive' Ed for all her past hurts and decided instead to have an affair herself, selfishly pursuing her own passions. Ed found out about her affair and then could not forgive Jan for her betrayal to him. Both had become so consumed with their anger and resentment that it became impossible to understand each others' perspective, let alone how their children must have been feeling in all of this mess.

What is love?

'Keep love in your heart. A life without it is like a sunless garden where the flowers are dead. The consciousness of loving and being loved brings warmth and richness to life that nothing else can bring' Oscar Wilde

Ed and Jan had always said to me that they had fallen madly in love with each other when they first met and that they were still in love. Yet that didn't mean that they had a genuinely good relationship. Falling in love gives a romantic relationship its electricity or chemistry. Millions of us devote a huge amount of time and effort to the search for romantic love. Love is the subject of millions of songs, films, books and plays. Internet dating agencies and singles events are full of people in search for someone to 'love'. Some people have regarded love to be so crucial to them that they have been prepared to cheat, steal, and even murder in its name. Love seems to be the route to everlasting happiness. But is it?

There are, in fact, different types of 'love':

'**Falling In Love**' is the one we all romanticize about happening and is the one that songs and poems are written about. It makes us feel ecstatically happy and happens due to a combination of intense sexual attraction, passion, electricity, sensuality, and merging. The hormone responsible for this love is Oxytocin. Oxytocin is best known for its roles in female reproduction. It is released in large amounts during labor, and after stimulation of the nipples, facilitating birth and breastfeeding. Recent studies have begun to investigate oxytocin's role in various behaviors, including orgasm and pair bonding. We enjoy needing, and being needed by, the other person and giving and receiving deep affection and intimacy. There should, however, be a warning that this love often renders you slightly insane and is more often than not merely transitional. **So why are we so strongly attracted to 'falling in love?** Why does this love seem so intense and passionately ecstatic, energised and happily omnipotent?

The reason that we 'consciously' are attracted to someone is usually because they are similar to us in some basic way, be it class, religion, money, looks, shared interests or some other similarity in background or values. This reminds us of past, familiar feelings of love, and the pleasure and experiences that came with the love we had as children with our siblings and parents. There are also, however, much stronger attractions that are often inexplicable and which everyone calls the 'chemistry' or 'electricity' of love. This is more of an 'unconscious' attraction, which draws us to people with similar unconscious issues to ourselves. These may include past experiences, happy or traumatic, or current unconscious passions, ambitions, drives and needs all of which we shall call 'baggage'. The couple passionately 'in love' with each other are not therefore usually aware of each other's 'baggage', or may even be slightly aroused by it. But as time goes on, more often than not those past hurts are recreated.

Many a tearful client has arrived at my couch with a sad story to tell about this.

Emma had been constantly bullied as a child and then as an adult was drawn to Robert, whom she liked for his strong personality. He said that all he wanted to do was to look after and care for her and that he knew what was best for her. This latter statement should have been a warning sign for Emma, but they had fallen in love and they got married. After the honeymoon period, however, Robert turned into a bully and once again Emma was re-living her childhood nightmare.

This is how cycles of negativity and damaging relationship patterns continue. Maybe, therefore, this passionate chemistry of 'falling in love' *should* have a government health warning attached to it! According to John Cleese and Robin Skynner in their book *'Families and How to Survive Them'*, this danger can be circumnavigated if the couple are willing to admit to, and to look at, what is in their baggage. They then become the best people to help each other deal with it, and through doing this the stage of deeper love can be reached.

__Ed__ had a hard time letting himself be loved. With overly busy, rather self-absorbed parents he had never really felt loved and connected to his family. Instead he had become a bit of a loner, seeking acceptance and approval only from his mates and work colleagues. This he carried through to adulthood. Jan too had busy parents and as part of a large family often felt left out. As an adult she often then felt shut out by Ed, as well as feeling unsupported while trying to get things 'right' with their children. She consciously craved the affection she had yearned for as a child and often felt very lonely and misunderstood by Ed. Paradoxically, her resentment of him and the lack of love and affection between them, served to recreate both their past hurts. What consoled Ed was his ability to escape to work, which he loved, and where as the boss he felt in control, appreciated and accepted. Jan, in contrast, shared her busy world with her kids, her friends and her own very close and supportive family. In many ways, therefore, Jan and Ed were quite dissimilar people with very different interests.

Other forms of love

'Platonic Love' involves a platonic affection and companionship that comes from friendships and family relationships.

'Object Love' involves loving material objects such as a new car or the latest dress .

'**Fantasy Love'** is the love of a famous or rich person or even a person that doesn't exist such as a movie figure or an internet 'avatar'. In this case the love is based on the individuals fantasy of what that person will be like. The whole drama of love can be played out safely in the mind. This type of love can of be an innocent teenage past time, whilst awaiting REAL love, but it can also be much more sinister resulting in 'stars' being stalked in their everyday life, which can lead to acute distress for the individual concerned or worse to their murder such as the case of John Lennon.

Is love amongst celebrities any different to normal love?

Every day in the media we see celebrities falling in and out of love with the speed of lightening. Probably most mentioned are the love stories around the likes of Katie Price, Kerry Katona or Russell Brand. So why does love seem to happen so easily and so often for celebrities? Being within the glitzy media celebrity society, gives these 'stars' so many opportunities for all of the different types of magical love - the 'falling in love' love, the platonic love, the object love and the fantasy love whilst their relationships rarely last long enough to develop into the more rational deeper love. Platonic relationships, within the intense atmosphere of the movie or stage set and the added fantasy factor of the characters they are playing soon can turn into the beginnings of 'celebrity love'. Then there are the fantastically extravagant celebrity parties, with all the 'beautiful people' involved (attractively painted and attired celebs with a dash of hyperactivity, passion and narcissism). Add this to the lure of glittering object love of their gemstones, ultra chic fashion garments and flashy cars and finish off with a cocktail of unlimited alcohol and mountains of drugs and you have the makings of 'celebrity love'. The result of this love is usually a series of illicit passionate affairs, rushed marriages and a flurry of 'celebrity love' children. And when life gets too real and maybe a little too boring for the celebs then along come more celebrity engagements, with more 'beautiful' people, always ready to replenish their aspirations for 'perfect' love. Hence more 'celebrity love', more celebrity break ups and more 'love children' scattered along the way. Is this that different to normal love. Not really. Just a lot quicker.

'Deeper Love' grows as the falling in love stage wanes and our sanity returns. This stage involves the huge effort of caring deeply for one another and supporting and nurturing each other's growth. This can be both intimate and sexual within a romantic relationship or platonic within a family relationship or friendship.

Similarity amongst partners is an important factor for a good relationship.

A red rose is not selfish because it wants to be a red rose. It would be horribly selfish if it wanted all the other flowers in the garden to be both red and roses. Oscar Wilde

The old saying is that 'opposites attract'. But they don't necessarily stay together! Studies have found that couples who stay together longer are more similar to one another than those who do not. The similarities uncovered included physical attractiveness, career plans, intelligence and age.

Traditionally, family matchmaking ensured that a good 'match' was made at the expense of passionate love. 'Free love' then developed from the mid-20th century, when families had little influence on finding partners for their offspring. During this time, the unconscious 'chemistry' of love took precedence in finding a partner. After numerous failed 'in love' relationships, many people are now voluntarily, albeit rather sheepishly, turning away from this rather barmy, haphazard and frankly risky type of 'love seeking'. Instead they are returning to a more sensible form of matchmaking, most notably through Internet dating sites. These sites match profiles, which document our personalities, values, religious beliefs, interests, hobbies, children and financial circumstances in as much detail as we care to share. This match is then intended to lead to 'love' that is perhaps less passionate, but is certainly a more stable and 'deeper love', ensuring that these two people will become long-term friends, loving companions and soul mates, as well as partners and parents.

Janice and Tony met 20 years ago, via a computer-dating site (internet wasn't available then). Both had been in unsuccessful relationships and were still single by their mid-30s. They had become disheartened with the dating game and decided to use the computer dating agency as an alternative. They were surprised when they met each other how much they already had in common. They had different jobs but were both employed in a caring profession. They loved doing many of the same things, such as going on caravanning or camping holidays. They both had had difficult childhoods within broken families, and had decided therefore not to marry or to have children but instead to enjoy and focus on their own relationship. Now in their 50s, they have never regretted their decision to look for a partner in this way. Both feel that they are each other's best friend, although they have a lot of their own friends, and mutual friends, as well. They confide in one another about everything and love each other very much. They are both friendly, positive people who very much value how they have spent their lives together thus far.

Similarity must not, however, be attained through unnatural identification, or through imposing similarities on another. This often happens when one half of the couple is either over-dependent or over-dominant.

Bob and Cynthia were like this. Bob had grown up in a very traditional family, where his dad had been the boss both at work and at home. Bob had followed his father in running the family business and naturally he felt that he should also be the boss at home. This meant that he wanted things done his way, which he felt was naturally the right way. Cynthia had been brought up in a more modern family, where her parents shared most of the management of the household, and naturally she expected the same dynamic in her own marriage. She had therefore found her relationship with Bob extremely undermining, frustrating and upsetting, and she had become overweight through comfort eating. Bob, in his own frustration, had told Cynthia she was fat, unattractive and miserable, and that she should go to the doctor to get a diet sheet and some anti-depressants. Fortunately the doctor referred her to me and we looked at the traditional roles that she and Bob had adopted, as well as the differences generally between men and women.

Do men and women really come from different planets?

Despite matching ensuring similar social and cultural backgrounds there can still be many differences in mixed gender relationships, which are based purely on the psychological and physical differences between men and women.

Women tend to be more intuitive, caring, empathic, intimate, sharing, tactful, gentle, passive and dependent whilst men are traditionally more status-conscious, independent, dominant, confident, ambitious, competitive and aggressive. Men have traditionally adopted the rational and authoritative role, as well as being the provider, whilst women have adopted the emotional role of family carer, housewife and communicator. By way of a biological explanation of how these roles emerged, female sex hormones, oestrogen and progesterone, fluctuate within a woman's normal monthly cycle, pregnancy and the menopause. This causes a rollercoaster effect on the female mood, physiology and energy levels. Men are influenced by their sex hormone, testosterone, which makes them physically stronger than women but also more prone to aggression, which means historically they have been the ones who have gone out and hunted for food.

Having made these gender comparisons, it is important, however, to acknowledge that, over the last century, changes in social thinking mean that gender roles have changed dramatically. Men are increasingly staying at home with the children whilst women are working more outside of the home. Family responsibility and management is now more often than not shared between the two partners, especially if both of them go out to work. With more enlightened and equal parenting and schooling, and with a more accepting society, women have become more confident and less passive and dependent, while men are no longer embarrassed to be more emotional and empathic. The sexes are now, therefore, more equal than they have ever been, and share the same desire for love, excitement, challenges, competition and success.

Check the similarities and differences between you and your partner through looking at each of your parent's relationships

We have mentioned briefly how Jan and Ed were influenced by their childhood. We can tell a lot about our own relationships by looking also at the relationship that our parents had. If we think about the issues each of them had with each other and what their values (cultural, religious or political) were, then we can compare them with our own issues and values. Let's look at Jan's and Ed's parents' relationship history.

Jan's parent's relationship history	*Ed's parent's relationship history*
Constant rowing about time and money.	*Constant rowing about time and money.*
Noisy chaotic household – 3 kids close in age.	*Orderly household with 2 kids.*
Mother more dominant at home.	*Father more dominant at home.*
Both parents shared financial responsibility.	*Father controlled finances.*
Both worked – father's busy job was considered more important than mother's part-time one	*Both worked full time – father's job considered more important (he often worked 7 days a week).*

Mother resentful of father's work involvement.

Had shared interests such as dancing, wine or going out together or with kids.

Never divorced.

Mother resentful of father's work involvement.

Had very separate interests – mum loved bridge and dad either working or going to pub with his work colleagues.

Never divorced.

Jan's relationship history

Had successful career when they met.

First marriage failed.

Jan was more passive after kids born

Jan worked part-time to look after kids and became resentful of Ed's long hours away from home.

Jan wanted equal management of finances.

Jan did not make time for individual interests and wanted to do everything together.

Did not feel divorce was an option.

Ed's relationship history

Had his own business working 7 days a week.

First marriage failed

Ed was more dominant after kids arrived.

Ed cut down his excessive work hours under pressure from Jan, but he felt resentful of this.

Ed wanted sole control of finances.

Ed made too much time for individual interests and liked to go to pub with mates after work.

Did not feel divorce was an option.

Both Jan and Ed rowed constantly, just as their parents had, about money and time. They stuck the marriage out without considering divorce, which seemed an unthinkable option. This is how they ended up in the aforementioned predicament of resentment, frustration and infidelity.

Perhaps you could compare yours and your partner's parent's relationship history with your own relationship histories and see if, like Jan and Ed there is a striking similarity.

Equality in relationships

It is important that a relationship be fair and equitable. Inequality leads to a mixture of negative emotions such as resentment, anger, guilt and discontentment, which is exactly what Jan and Ed experienced within their relatively unequal relationship. Ed had felt it was right that he controlled their household finances, just like his own dad had done, and he felt acute frustration and resentment that Jan constantly challenged this.

Getting the right amount of dependency in relationships

Over-dependent people desperately seek to be loved by others in order to fill up the emptiness they feel within themselves. When other people are not available to fill that void, they look towards other substitutes, such as over-indulging in food, alcohol or drugs and other obsessive or addictive behaviours. Over-dependent people rarely feel happy or fulfilled. This is because they have little knowledge of who they really are and instead define themselves by who they are with, or what they can do for others. They cling to bad relationships through a lack of belief in themselves. They passively look to others, even their own children, as the source of their happiness and fulfilment, and therefore when they are not happy then they are disappointed in, or blame, those people. Over-dependency may, therefore, appear to be 'love', but it is not. It depletes rather than nurtures the people they 'love'. So too can over-independent people destroy a relationship, by not allowing the person they 'love' to enter their world at all, leading to feelings of isolation for both parties.

Jan and Ed had realised, through therapy, that Jan had become over-dependent in their relationship, whilst Ed had been overly independent and somewhat controlling.

Change happening in relationships

Carl Rogers says, '*We are all in a state of becoming*' and so within a relationship we will inevitably change and grow, both individually and together. But if this change occurs more apparently in one partner than the other, then it can also cause problems.

Jan changed after Ed's affair. She decided to return to the career ambitions and interests that she had before having children. But in order to do this, she had to ask Ed to contribute more time to the family. He was unhappy about this, as he felt his career was more important than hers and was reluctant to change. Eventually, along with the cumulative effect brought about by Jan's affair, their different interests and priorities led to their separation and divorce. After Jan and Ed's divorce, however, each began to see the other as an individual, once more, with their own interests and careers. They began to respect each other again, just as they had done when they first met. Jan said, 'After the divorce, somehow, the pressure was off. We didn't have any expectations anymore. And we found out that we really did like each other again'. Although it was too late for them to get back together again, they became friends rather than constant adversaries, as they had been when married.

Whom being loved is poor? Oscar Wilde

Many of us, either consciously or unconsciously, define our lives and attachments by the question *What do I own?* rather than *Whom do I love?* The second question can, however, help us step off the materialistic, consumerist treadmill and put our attachment energy back into the relationships that really matter – with people, not products.

When we define ourselves by '*what do I own?*', we're essentially saying '*I am what I own*'. In contrast, '*whom do I love?*' inspires us to look into our hearts to find out who we are, rather than at the material attachments that surround us. When we further ask ourselves '*what am I worth?*' some immediately interpret this as 'what do I own', whilst others define it as 'I am worth their love'. Defining ourselves by 'whom do I love' we can then replace egotism with altruism, compassion and humility, caring as much about our loved ones as we do about ourselves.

Love map

A love map is a large circle, with 3 or 4 concentric circles within it. You are the dot in the middle of the innermost circle. The first circle represents all the people you feel closest to, whom you love, who love you and who are most important to you. These may or may not be your parents, your siblings, your children, your partner, your lover or your friends. Then in the next circle represents those who are next closest to you and so on, until the fourth circle contains those who you are only loosely connected with. Think about how much of your time you spend with each of those people and decide whether this proportion of time is appropriate to their importance in your life.

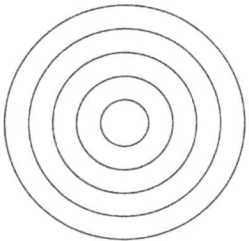

Exercise 6 – who you loved

Think about what or who you loved:

People I loved as a child:
Who made you feel most safe and loved e.g. parents, grandparent, sibling, neighbour, who played a central role in your life?

Places I loved as a child:
Where did you feel most safe and connected e.g. tree house, bedroom, in front of the tv?

Objects I loved to as a child:
What things made you feel most safe and connected e.g dolls, animals, blankets etc?

People I have fallen in Love with as an adult:
List all the times you have fallen madly in love with someone

People I love(d) platonically as an adult
List colleagues, friends and family whom you love platonically

James *came to talk to me when he had experienced his colleague and close friend suddenly dying whilst at work of a heart attack. He was very concerned that his colleague had spent so long at work and travelling that had not been able to spend very much time with his family. James realised that he was doing the same thing. He drew the love map and this proved that he spent most time with his work colleagues and in his need for intimacy, had somehow turned them into his new family. He decided to start looking for a job that was closer to his family and where he did not have to travel so much.*

10 tips on improving genuinely loving relationships

More has been written about how relationships don't work, than about how they do. Somehow the thought of happy relationships seems at worst sickening and at best rather mythical. I would, therefore, like to write about how relationships can work.

1. Relationships require enormous effort

The biggest secret of a successful relationship is effort, and a huge amount of it. Effort is required to make the relationship work every minute of every hour of every day. It's like luck – you are never just lucky, you have to work very hard at it. Working hard at it is about looking after yourself as well as looking after others. This may be in terms of nurturing yourself in terms of your body, your appearance and also your mind and your spirituality. But also in terms of nurturing others. Audrey Hepburn gave some great beauty tips:

Audrey Hepburn "beauty tips."
For attractive lips, speak words of kindness.For lovely eyes, seek out the good in people. For a slim figure, share your food with the hungry. For beautiful hair, let a child run his/her fingers through it once a day. For poise, walk with the knowledge that you never walk alone. People, even more than things, have to be restored, renewed, revived, reclaimed, and redeemed; never throw out anyone. Remember, if you ever need a helping hand, you will find one at the end of each of your arms. As you grow older, you will discover that you have two hands; one for helping yourself, and the other for helping others.

2. Build relationships based more on liking each other, rather than love

Although falling in love seems to be a magical experience, if two people are to spend a long time together then it is vital that they also like each other. The question is, could a relationship do without love if the couple like one another? Or could it do without liking each other if they love one another? Love without liking often leads to the 'I can't live with him but I can't live without him' cry for help. If, however, there is genuine liking and compatibility, then maybe a deeper love can develop.

3. Create positive energy in your relationships

A simple way of identifying whether you have the potential for lasting love in your relationship is by thinking of yourself, as well as those around you, in terms of energy. Look at your Love Map and decide whether your innermost people give you energy or draw energy from you. If you find that they draw so much energy from you that you often feel exhausted after being with them, then while they may profess to love you, in reality their love is more of an anti-love. Hopefully we choose friends whom we can both give energy to and draw energy from, but we are never so rational when it comes to choosing someone to love. Once, any imbalance is identified, then you can work on rebalancing it.

A client of mine, Michael, said that he felt absolutely exhausted all the time. He said that he had a loving and supportive wife and parents and a good job. I asked him what had been happening recently in his life and he told me that both his mother and his wife had been ill. His mother had developed dementia over the last year and he was having to support his father in her care. Also his wife had been diagnosed with breast cancer and had been having chemotherapy to treat this.

I explained to him that, whilst his family had normally been supportive and therefore energy giving, at this time they were drawing a lot of energy from him. He said that whilst he loved his job, it also had put more pressure on him due to some important contracts. I asked him who was able to give him energy at this time and he looked blankly at me. We looked at how he could look up some of his best friends that could support and re-energise him. He also agreed that coming to see me helped increase his energy during this difficult time.

4. Retain individuality whilst integrating your inner male and female

Retaining ones individuality is of utmost importance for a successful relationship with another person. Being healthily selfish is not wrong, as many people believe it to be. We are individuals and our personalities are never meant to merge. We can, however, merge our own male and female inner selves. Males can merge with some of female nurturer within them, whilst females can merge with some of the male provider and risk-taker within them. This has happened over the last 40 years with the rise of feminism and the subsequent re-writing of gender roles and attributes for both sexes.

5. Communicate effectively with each other

Most relationship breakdowns happen after a communication breakdown. If you can keep up the lines of effective communication, then you have a much better chance of resolving any issues yourselves. Effective communication means clarity, focus, non-defensiveness and support for your partner.

- Take responsibility for yourself.
- Let your partner take responsibility for herself/himself.

- Don't enter into a win/lose argument.
- Turn all complaints/criticisms into requests.
- Distinguish opinion from fact.
- Avoid emotional absolutes like 'always' and 'never'.
- Catch yourself – learn to identify when you're acting out of destructive and negative patterns of behaviour, and stop yourself.

6. Use sex as a currency for intimacy

This is the catch 22 in relationship sex: Men generally become more emotionally intimate when they have had sex (think of the post-coital intimate conversations you have had), whilst women generally want to have sex once they have felt emotionally intimate with their partner. How often have you had great sex after having resolved a huge argument or shared a deeply emotional experience? Sex may, therefore, simply be the currency for emotional intimacy within a relationship. Perhaps only when we practise true emotional intimacy can we express ourselves sexually without selfishness, manipulation, competition or resentment.

What turns you on? Having fun is just about as important as living, and sexy fun is part of that living. It's pleasurable, it's intimate, it's good exercise, it can make you laugh and it increases the levels of your 'natural high' chemicals such as endorphins and adrenaline. Find out what turns you on and what turns your partner on. Get all those sexy books out, or the videos. Anything goes, as long as it safe and agreeable to you both. If you enjoy being gently massaged, then get the oils out; if you or your partner love oral sex, do it - and add a bit of chocolate just for fun.

Each sexual partner can create their own menu of 'sexual tastes' and agree a price for each taste depending on the effort required! That in itself often breaks down any sexual inhibitions, as well as often producing raucous laughter. Then each partner can pick from their menu and create debit and credit accounts accordingly! If one partner is always in debit and the other massively in credit then there is something rather imbalanced about their sex life.

7. Nurture your relationship
Nurture your relationship that is based not only on love but also on better communication and more joy, compassion, honesty and openness, with less resentment and fewer negative emotions.

8. Respect
Respect that each partner is responsible for themselves. That each has a shared responsibility for their family, as well as a wider responsibility for their career and their community. Also respect each other's individual differences, interests and needs.

9. Do it Now

Deal with issues now, before they build up and before you become too emotional and resentful.

10. A Contract of love and mutual respect

In order to keep a genuinely loving relationship it is worth each signing up to a contract of love and mutual respect.

Comes the Dawn Veronica A. Shoffstal

After a while you learn a subtle difference
Between holding a hand and chaining a soul.
And you learn that love doesn't mean leaning
And company doesn't mean security,
And you begin to learn that kisses aren't contracts
And presents aren't promises,
And you begin to accept your defeats
With your head up and your eyes open,
With the grace of a woman, not the grief of a child.
And you learn to build all your roads on today
Because tomorrow's ground is too uncertain for plans.
And futures have a way of falling down mid-flight.
After a while you learn
That even sunshine burns if you get too much.
So you plant your own garden and decorate your own soul,

Instead of waiting for someone to bring you flowers.
And you learn that you really can endure...
That you really are strong,
And you really do have worth
And you learn and you learn...
With every goodbye you learn.

4. Dare to Laugh & be Happy

> You alone have the capacity to choose your response to life. When you form the habit of searching for the positive, empowering event in every circumstance in your life you will move into its higher dimensions and you will banish worry forever. You will stop being a prisoner of your past. Instead you will become the architect of your future.' The Monk Who Sold His Ferrari – Robin Sharma

Being happy is defined as being content or fortunate, yet those moments of happiness are rarely permanent as we, ourselves are never permanent.

Happiness, like love, is priceless and yet so many people have spent fortunes seeking it. Yet it, like love comes in different forms.

Some people like Elvis Presley have pursued happiness at all costs, through seeking ultimate pleasure, satisfaction and excitement. Others like Dalai Lama seek happiness through wisdom, understanding, authenticity and integrity; through having positive, loving relationships and accepting oneself; through autonomy; through feeling in charge of ones life; and through personal growth and purpose in life. Hopefully by the time you have read this chapter you will be able to decide which type of happiness you wish to pursue.

Elvis Presley and his daring for happiness

Elvis Presley, after the loss of his dearly beloved mother, pursued happiness through excessive hedonism. He spent most of his time constantly seeking new and stimulating sources of pleasure, as documented by Albert Goldman in his book 'Elvis'. Goldman wrote that Elvis' motto was 'Take it to the max!' He rapidly became bored with most things, but his wealth and fame gave him great scope for taking things to extremes. He developed a special taste for junk food. On one occasion Elvis and his friends decided they wanted a certain type of sandwich, so they all flew off to Denver from Memphis, with the return trip plus sandwiches costing around £20,000. He threw parties for 40 or 50 girls and only 7 or 8 men. The girls had to be pretty, no older than 18, no taller than 5'2", and weigh no more than 110 pounds. If he wanted a plane he bought himself 4. If he wanted a car he bought 14 brand new Cadillac's. Despite all this he still remained in despair when he died, aged 42, having taken over 12 different drugs in large doses, at a weight of around 18 stone.

Suffering can temporarily destroy happiness

In a way it was, therefore, Elvis' suffering from the grief of his mother's death that started his pursuit of happiness.

The Dalai Lama, author of *The Art of Happiness* states his simple formula for increasing happiness, *'Increase the factors that cause you happiness and decrease the factors that cause you suffering'*. Feeling initial shock, despair, trauma or grief, it is hard to imagine that any positive outcome could ever come out of it. But from my experience of helping survivors work through their personal tragedies, most have eventually found some form of positive growth and eventual happiness.

__Karen,__ aged 42, had always been quite negative about life, and felt that she was generally unhappy. She took drugs and drank alcohol to try to feel happier, but the after-effects would just send her deeper into depression. She was also one of life's great moaners, and felt as if life had never treated her 'fairly'. She had experienced a bad relationship where she was bullied and hit regularly. She had tried different businesses but somehow they always failed. She just felt that things never went her way. Then worst of all, she found out she had breast cancer. She became even more depressed at the thought of having surgery and chemotherapy. She had always been attractive and the thought of losing her hair and one of her breasts seemed to upset *her more than the idea of losing her life. But then, faced with the gradual reality of a potentially limited life ahead of her, she starting thinking about how important life was to her. During the chemotherapy she began to value the life that she did have left. Just after her operation, whilst still recovering in hospital, she met other cancer patients, many much younger than her. There was one person whom she grew particularly close to, and to whom she continued to visit in hospital after she herself had left. That friend eventually died of cancer, at only 28 years old.*

It was at this point that Karen decided that she really wanted to fight for her own life and that, if she was lucky enough to survive, she would live life to the full. She has since done exactly that and has engaged in life and loved it. She has resumed her jewellery business and created a beautiful new range. She has also been busy fundraising for her local cancer unit. She said that in many ways her cancer has been the best thing that has happened to her and that she has been happier than ever before.

*When I saw **Sally**, already mentioned in chapter 2, after her husband's memorial service she was still extremely upset and bereft. She was haunted by the horrific image of him behind that glass looking at her. She had been feeling suicidal, yet unable to ask for help. In our session I asked her if she could put herself in her husband's place on that fateful day. Who would have been the last person he would have wanted to see as he died?*

How would he have wanted her to live after his death? Sally realised how fortunate she and her husband had been, in that moment, to be able to express their love for each other. She also realised how lucky she had been to survive and also how strong she must have been to fight against the huge weight of water when going up the stairs.

I helped her to turn her negative despair and helplessness into positive strength and hope; to take forward what her husband would have wanted for her - to survive, to go back to their home and to carry on with her career and eventually become happy once more. I reminded her of a poem, 'She is Gone' by David Harkins, which had been read out at the Memorial service but I changed it slightly to relate to her own circumstances.

She is Gone – David Harkins
You can shed tears that I have gone, or you can smile because I lived
You can close your eyes and pray I will come back, or you can open your eyes and
see all I have left behind.
Your heart can be empty because you cannot see me, or you can be full of the love I shared with you.
You can turn your back on tomorrow and live yesterday, or you can be happy for tomorrow because of yesterday.

You can remember me and only that I have gone, or you can cherish my memory and
let it live on.
You can cry and close your mind, be empty and turn your back, or you can do what I
would want – smile, open your eyes, love and go on."

When have you felt happy and why?

When we are happy, we are always good, but when we are good we are not always happy - Oscar Wilde

Before we attempt to understand what happiness is, perhaps it would be a good idea to look at what has already caused us to be happy or unhappy in the past and how we have contributed to this.

Exercise 7 – happy and unhappy times

Think about your happiest times and your unhappiest times when looking at these questions. I have included some of my own examples.

Your happiest times

1. When were you at your happiest? E.g. When I was on holiday
2. Where were you at your happiest? E.g. Being by the sea and in the sunshine
3. Who were you with when happiest? E.g. When I was with my family.

4.   What were you happiest doing? Eg. Sailing, ski-
      ing or simply taking my dog for a walk in the sun
5.   How did external influences make you happy?
      E.g. Good feedback from my work/friends/family
6.   How did you make yourself happy? E.g. Work-
      ing and having fun with my friends and family.

Your unhappiest times

1.   When were you at your unhappiest? E.g. Just
      after my second marriage broke up
2.   Where were you at your unhappiest? E.g. In
      London feeling isolated, humiliated or belittled
3.   Who were you with when unhappiest? E.g.
      With arrogant or insensitive people
4.   What were you unhappiest doing? E.g. Doing
      something against my values and beliefs
5.   How did external influences make you un-
      happy? E.g. Getting unhelpful negative feed-
      back or losing trust with a loved one
6.   How did you make yourself unhappy? E.g.
      Being with people who belittle me or do not
      value me

Perhaps you may now be getting an idea of what you feel
has made you happy or unhappy in the past and whether
there has been a pattern to your unhappiness. Perhaps
you have somehow drawn yourself into unhappiness or
repeated past mistakes. Or you may have tragically faced
crises in life of which you have had to overcome.

Exercise 8 – happiness chart

If you were to plot your life experiences on your chart of life, at your various ages, in terms of happiness on a scale of + 5 to -5, where 5 is most happy and -5 is least happy, would it mostly positive or mostly negative?

Happy   **Happiness Chart**

+5

+4

+3

+2

+1

0 ....

-1

-2

-3

-4

-5

    5 10 15 20 25 30 35 40 45 50 55 60 65 70

Unhappy   **Age**

What is Happiness?

The Dalai Lama's Art of Happiness

Despite the Dalai Lama's simple formula for happiness, many of us still seem to voluntarily draw suffering onto ourselves whilst generally avoiding doing the things that make us happy. The Dalai Lama says that he increases his own happiness through his willingness to reach out to others and to create a feeling of affinity and goodwill, even in the briefest of encounters. Happiness, he says, is determined more by one's state of mind than by external events and is, therefore, a very individual thing. Until relatively recently we have not had the chemical technology (neurobiology) to explain our complex brain and body changes, and we have historically explained our happiness in philosophical, sociological or psychological terms.

Philosophical explanation of happiness

Philosophers, Aristotle, Hippocrates and Plato all stated that moderation and balance was what was the key to a happy and harmonious life. Aristotle wrote that man can only achieve happiness through using all of his abilities and capabilities. He said that the three contributors to happiness must be present simultaneously, and in balance for true happiness and fulfilment to be achieved. He cited these three factors as being:

- pleasure and enjoyment
- life as a free and responsible citizen
- life as a thinker and philosopher

The philosopher Nietzsche wrote 'For happiness, how little suffices for happiness!... the least thing precisely, the gentlest thing, the lightest thing, a lizard's rustling, a breath, a wisk, and eye glance – little maketh up the best happiness. Be still'.

Most people, in their restless search for something significant to happen to them, continuously miss the insignificant, which may not be insignificant at all.

Sociological explanation of happiness

A National Opinion Poll (NOP) by GfK (Gesellschaft für Konsumforschung market research company 2005) provided anecdotal evidence of what makes us happy.

Love and Relationships - It has been proven that people who are in love are at their happiest – at least for the period that they are 'in love'. When they are 'in love' they feel particularly positive and optimistic and create the happy mood messenger Serotonin. Nearly half of married people reported that they are "very happy". Only a quarter of singles said the same. Researchers believe the key factor is the promise to stay together.

Almost half the people surveyed (48%) said that relationships are the biggest factor in making them happy. Yet most of us speak to only a small number of close friends every week. 6 out of 10 people spoke to 5 friends or fewer each week. 2 out of 10 spoke to only 1 or 2 friends. And 1 person in 25 talked to no friends at all.

Health - 24% of the poll believed that good health was the next biggest factor in making people happy. Among those who described themselves as "very happy", 45% said they had "very good" health. Among those only "fairly happy" 23% said they had "very good" health.

Wealth - The poll provides the first evidence that Britain's happiness levels are declining - a trend already well documented in the United States. The proportion of people saying they are "very happy" has fallen from 52% in 1957 to just 36% today. In America social scientists have seen levels of life satisfaction gradually decline over the last quarter of a century. In the early 1970s, 34% of those interviewed in the General Social Survey described themselves as "very happy". By the late 1990s, the figure was 30% - a small but statistically significant drop. Wealth therefore fails to translate into happiness in the Western world. What the happiness research suggests is that once average incomes reach about £10,000 a year, extra money does not make people any happier.

Where you live in the world - Many different organisations, including the United Nations, have attempted to compare the happiness rates of different countries. A recent poll asked people how satisfied they were with their lives as a whole, using a one to 10 scale. Switzerland was the happiest country, followed by Denmark, Sweden, Ireland and the USA with Britain coming eighth.

Psychological explanations of happiness

There are many different fields of psychology that have their explanations of happiness. Let us look at a few of the important ones.

Psychotherapists and Psychoanalysts believe that happiness and unhappiness arise from past experiences or traumas. **Freud** said that love and work is what gives people happiness and satisfaction whilst **Jung** said that the basic elements needed by humans in order to be happy were:

- Good physical and mental health;
- Good personal and intimate relationships;
- The faculty for perceiving beauty in art and nature;
- Reasonable standards of living and satisfactory work;
- A philosophic or religious point of view, capable of coping with life's unpredictability.

Behaviourists explain that happiness and unhappiness arise out of learned behaviour and they concentrate on changing behaviour to improve happiness. These could include going for a walk, jogging, cycling dancing or singing. We will, later, look at some activities that can make us happy.

Cognitive psychologists explain that happiness/unhappiness might arise from learned thoughts and ways of thinking so they work on changing these to increase happiness. By accepting that both fortunate and unfortunate things happen in life, we can begin to view each experience, good or bad, rationally, as something that will help us broaden our life experience, rather than destroy it. They believe that whatever you are doing should be as enjoyable as it can possibly be. If you focus too closely or intensely on a problem when it occurs, it may seem overwhelming. But if you have a wider perspective to national or global levels then the problem never seems so important.

Life is much too important a thing to talk seriously about - Oscar Wilde - we live in a world where many people take themselves and their decisions far too seriously. We can easily 'awfulize' a situation or feel a victim of circumstances by having a heightened sense of our own importance. If we lose most or all of our money through unfortunate business dealings, or our marriage breaks up, or we lose a loved one, the negative emotions can escalate into the PLOM (poor little old me) mentality. We can then become seriously unhappy, as a result feeling (irrationally) that the world is not fair and that everything bad happens to us. *Or* we can change the way we view our circumstances and be lighter and laugh more about it. Whilst we are also increasingly surrounded by stress, we can be more resilient towards it by changing how we perceive it. We will be looking more into this in chapter 7.

Biological explanations of happiness

Recent advances in neurobiology has enabled studies to show that our moods, thoughts and physicality are all very much interdependent between our brain and body chemistry. We have communication systems of electrical and chemical mood messengers within our central nervous system, which dictates to our body and mind how to react to given situations and experiences. This gives us our enormous versatility and complexity of moods which effects our happiness, pain, pleasure, emotions, anxiety, appetite, memory, sleep, alertness, stress, depression and general health.

Our 'happy' mood messengers, Serotonin, for example, seems to enhance our feelings of security, courage, assertiveness, self-worth, calm, flexibility and resilience. Deficiencies of Serotonin have been linked to dips in mood and other psychological disorders such as depression and anxiety. The precise role played by Serotonin, and whether it acts independently or with other neurotransmitters, is not fully clear. In minor depression, a feeling of security and support may be sufficient to alleviate symptoms, whilst in major depression, a more specific talking and drug treatment may be necessary.

Through understanding more about our brain and body chemistry, we may be able to make more knowledgeable decisions regarding how we can maximise our happiness. This will be looked at more in Chapter 6.

Ten pathways for pursuing happiness

Pursuing happiness from food, alcohol or drugs can certainly seem to be the ultimate quick fix but then most quick fixes don't last long and can lead to unhealthy craving and ultimate unhappiness. Let us have a look at each one in turn.

1. Happiness through food

High glycaemic value (HGV) carbohydrate foods create our 'happy' mood messenger, Serotonin. These include all forms of sugar, honey, syrups, alcohol, potatoes, corn and refined foods such as white flour and white rice - more commonly known as junk food. Chocolate contains these rapid release carbohydrates, which is why we reach for the chocolate as soon as we feel 'low' and want to increase our happiness. We will be looking further into this subject in Chapter 6.

2. Happiness through alcohol

Work is the curse of the drinking classes - Oscar Wilde
Alcohol is used all over the world in the pursuit of happiness, relaxation and confidence

'I feel great when I'm drunk'

Tim would go out to get drunk because he felt 'low' and needed to escape all his day to day stresses. Drinking alcohol did the trick and he felt happy, energetic and uninhibited for the duration of the evening. He became the life and soul of the party and had a fantastic time with his friends, who all thought he was a great laugh.

For every person who opposes 'the demon drink' there is an ardent supporter like Tim. Alcohol's ability to improve our mood, as well as being enjoyable, has made it popular with over 90% of adults in Britain. The effect of alcohol, as well as those of other drugs, depends on our expectations as individuals, as well as of the chemical reaction it will trigger in our brains. Because alcohol can lower inhibitions, people can be affected very differently, depending on what their differing inhibitions are. Many people find that they say or do things that wouldn't normally. The Romans coined the phrase, 'In Vino Veritas' ('in wine there is truth'). For those of us who feel sexually inhibited, alcohol seems to relax us and help us feel more aroused and stimulated, although chemically it does not act as an arousal or stimulant, but as a depressant. Perhaps this is the reason alcohol is called 'spirit'.

There is even evidence to suggest that those who drink moderate amounts of alcohol are less likely to suffer from coronary heart disease, and have fewer colds!

Although alcohol can be classed as a drug, it has hardly ever, at least in the western world, been made completely illegal. America is the exception to this rule, having had a period of prohibition in the 1930s. Unfortunately, instead of wiping alcohol out of American society, prohibition facilitated the growth of a huge illicit industry!

There are many people in the world, however, for whom alcohol is taboo, such as Muslims and Mormons. Muslims are forbidden to drink it, on the basis of Mohammed's displeasure when he discovered his troops drunk on the eve of a battle. Mormons and other Christian sects find plenty of reasons for abstaining from alcohol - it is addictive; it causes illness; it ruins lives; it leads to violent behaviour in young people; and it is a major cause of death on the roads.

The alcoholic roller coaster ride

*After a night of 'fun and frivolity', **Tim** found that the next morning would hit him like a ton of bricks. As well as realising that his problems were still there, he had a headache and felt even more miserable and tired. After taking pills for his headache, he then felt he needed more food or even alcohol, in order to feel good again. Bit like a roller coaster isn't it? One that ends in misery, exhaustion and ill-health.*

As well as reducing our inhibitions enabling us to have more fun, alcohol can also release our hidden darker side. Were alcohol to be discovered today, its sale would never be permitted because of its potentially lethal side-effects. Alcohol causes us to become overconfident of our abilities, but also slower to react. Our speech becomes slurred, our balance becomes impaired and we can lose our ability to remember things. Too much alcohol, for a man, can cause impotence. Very large amounts can induce coma or even death! By far the most common danger associated with drinking alcohol is injury in accidents. Perhaps by understanding the following tips about alcohol you could, unlike the Middle Eastern pleasure boat disaster, enjoy consuming alcohol without capsizing yourself!

10 tips for understanding alcohol

1. *As well as reducing our inhibitions enabling us to have more fun, alcohol can also release our hidden darker side.* Were alcohol to be discovered today, its sale would never be permitted because of its potentially lethal side-effects. Alcohol causes us to become overconfident of our abilities, but also slower to react.

2. *Alcohol can cause our* speech becomes slurred, our balance becomes impaired and we can lose our ability to remember things.

3. *Too much alcohol, for a man, can cause impotence.* A term often called Brewers droop.

4. *Very large amounts can induce coma or even death!* By far the most common danger associated with drinking alcohol is injury in accidents.

5. *Alcohol can give us a hangover* Most of the alcohol we drink is processed by our liver to form acetaldehyde, which has the effect of making us feel hot, headachy and nauseous.

6. *Alcohol can make us feel tired, irritable and depressed-* alcohol is chemically very

similar to sugar and therefore has the same effect of raising our blood sugar levels, creating the hypoglycaemic affect of feeling tired, irritable and depressed. This often induces the desire for another drink, promoting the addictive roller coaster lifestyle. Whilst a drink may help get us off to sleep, we are unlikely to get a good night's sleep, because alcohol deprives us of the early sleep in which we dream.

7. *Alcohol can lead to dehydration* - if we drink 250 mls of wine (about 2 units) we can lose at least 500 mls of water from our body as urine during the next two hours. This is because alcohol, prevents the kidneys giving the message to recycle water. The result is dehydration, unless this fluid is replaced by drinking plenty of water. Without fluids waste products and toxins build up and we can feel tired, headachy and constipated.

8. *Long term alcohol use can lead to obesity* - *a* unit of alcohol provides us with about 70 calories, although beer and wine has a lot more calories especially if drunk in large quantities. Although alcohol is high in calories it does not supply energy or satisfy our desire for food in the way that carbohydrates can - indeed it seems to stimulate it. Alcohol therefore does little to help us work or exercise, but it can supply excess calories that lead to weight gain.

9. *Long term alcohol use can lead to ulcers, cirrhosis of the liver, depression and brain damage* - excess

alcohol can lead to acute inflammation of the stomach, especially if drunk on an empty stomach. Sustained heavy drinking of alcohol increases the risk of liver disease, particularly cirrhosis of the liver, various cancers, pancreatitis and ulcers. It can also lead to heart and circulation disorders, and even brain damage. Although short-term use may seem to alleviate depressive feelings, long-term drinking can increase depression.

10. ***Long term alcohol use can cause alcoholism*** - *after* prolonged and severe drinking, physiological and psychological dependence occurs (alcoholism). If alcohol consumption is then stopped, withdrawal symptoms occur such as restlessness, nausea, fever and hallucinations known as Delerium Tremens. In some cases, withdrawal produces such a profound shock to the body that it kills them. Alcoholism is believed to affect about 20 people in 10,000, and is more likely to affect women than men. What is more worrying, however, is the recent surge of binge drinking amongst the UK's population, particularly amongst the young, which could lead to longer term alcoholism.

3. Happiness through prescription or recreational drugs

Sometimes when we reach such a dead end of despair that we feel unable to cope on our own, then taking drugs, prescription or recreational may seem the only answer to improving our happiness.

Prescription drugs for happiness - prescription drugs include SSRI (Selective Serotonin Reuptake Inhibitor), type anti-depressants, such as Prozac which increase the amount of the happy messenger, Serotonin in our brain with very few side effects.

Recreational drugs for happiness - Ecstasy causes Serotonin to be released into our brain, making us feel calm, relaxed and happy, whilst Cannabis, in small amounts, produces a mild, pleasurable 'high', consisting of relaxation, a loss of social inhibition, intoxication, and humour.

4. Happiness through activity

'Do the things you have always wanted to do. Climb that mountain or learn that musical instrument or a new language. Love music and dance in the rain or build a new business. Rekindle the delight of your childhood. Stop putting off happiness for the sake of achievement. Revive your spirit and your soul.' The Monk Who Sold His Ferrari – Robin Sharma

Childish activity for happiness - do you remember when you were very small how easy it was for you to have fun, how you stamped your feet and screamed for what you wanted, how you played with any and every little thing you had in front of you, how easily you laughed? Naomi Wolf describes such a child in *Fire with Fire:*

'She could not keep still yet when she didn't want to move she would dig her heels into the floor and scream if picked up. If she wanted to keep her prized possession she clenched her fists so tightly around it as if her life depended on it. 'Mine' and 'You can't make me' were essential parts of her vocabulary. She gazed at her little body in the mirror for a long time, taking pleasure at seeing herself as she was, not as others wanted her to be. She was self absorbed yet sensitive and curious. She was fierce, greedy and egotistical yet she would easily shed a tear at my anguish. Her world was more saturated with passion, aspirations and ecstasy than it could ever be again. At her worst she was narcissistic and destructive; at her best, she was and still is the force of creativity, rebellion against injustice, and primal self-respect'. Naomi Wolf Fire with Fire

In the past many children have been so heavily conditioned, with restrictive rules and restraints that it has quashed their youthful exuberance and lust for life. They were taught that it is better to give up childish thoughts and selfish pleasures in favour of being adult, sensible and civilised. How often have you seen parents, who are with their children in the park, passively watching over them at their play, instead of playing and laughing with them. Actually participating in something rather than just observing is exciting, such as entering a race, driving, playing tennis, squash, pool, table tennis or cards.

High-risk activity for happiness - there is no doubt about it, high risk activity gets our adrenaline pumping. It doesn't really matter what we choose, as long as it is risky. These activities tend to be called extreme sports such, as bungee jumping, snow boarding or skydiving. Others may enjoy thrilling rides at theme parks. Perhaps with the absence of wars, we are drawn to adventure and risk.

Music, singing and dancing activity for happiness - music and dance has, throughout time, been both a hedonistic pleasure but also an important part of religious celebration and ritual. Early tribal dancing was performed in the open air, whilst medieval dancing was performed in castles, Viennese dancing in elegant ballrooms and Victorian dancing in parlours. This century has again seen great changes in music, and also great changes in both the style of dancing, When Bill Haley's film *Rock Around the Clock* came out in 1956, the kids were tossed around the ballroom doing the outrageous jive dancing or Rock 'n' Roll. Suddenly millions of people, irrespective of age, were buying portable transistor radios and began tapping their feet to the new beat and were looking for a suitable partner. Sadly the intimacy of couples dancing shifted, from the mid 60s to present day, to individual dancing, such as the Beatles twist or shake. Fortunately, TV programmes such as *Strictly Come Dancing* have re-introduced us to the art of dancing in couples, showcasing many different forms of dance from all over the world. All types of dancing, however, stimulate the dancer's happy mood messengers- adrenaline, endorphins and serotonin. Similarly singing or chanting can set off 24 curative hormones in the body.

Exercise for happiness - exercise will also create mood-enhancing messengers such as adrenaline and endorphins, which give us a feeling of euphoria. This is why so many people get hooked on exercise and why gyms and boot camps are so popular. Energetic activity can also relieve stress, decrease appetite and boost metabolic rate. There will be more on exercise in later chapters.

5. Happiness through entertainment - there can be the excitement of watching or listening to something stimulating, be it on television, in the cinema or in a theatre or music venue. It's a great feeling to have seen the most wonderful play, listened to the most enchanting music, or laughed at craziest of jokes.

6. Happiness through laughter
It has been proven in many research reports that laughter and smiling can increase your feel good factor chemicals. Even fake laughter or smiling can increase your endorphins and decrease your stress hormone cortisol (see YouTube 'Benefits of Laughter' by John Cleese). These chemicals will be explained more in Chapter 6. Studies have shown that children laugh up to 300 times a day whereas adults barely get to 20 times per day. As an adult, however, you can go to workshops

to learn how to feel great through laughter. A quick little exercise to get you started is to get out your mobile phone on a train or underground and pretend you have just heard the most amazing joke and laugh like crazy. Then look around and see how many others are trying to contain a smile. For those who prefer a more private laugh you can call a freephone number at 7am and listen to people laughing. If you think about it anything that makes you feel good – exercise, eating, sex, laughing, smiling etc moves your mouth from straight or down to lifted thus lifting your whole face. Try even that for 5 minutes and see how you feel good.

7. Happiness through smiling is a also wonderful positive affirmation both for yourself and for others. This anonymous poem always makes me smile:

Smiling is infectious - you catch it like the flu,
When someone smiled at me today I started smiling too.
I passed around the corner and someone saw my grin,
When he smiled, I realised I'd passed it on to him.
I thought about my smile and then I realised its worth.
A single smile like mine could travel right around the earth.
 If you feel a smile begin, don't leave it undetected,
Lets start an epidemic quick, and get the world infected
Anonymous

8. Happiness through love
As we have seen in Chapter 3, falling In Love can make us feel ecstatically happy, energised and

omnipotent. Films, plays, songs and poems are written about. It happens due to a combination of intense sexual attraction, passion, electricity, sensuality, and merging. But this type of happiness does not always last. A deeper and more profound love, humility and compassion not just for our partners and family but also for others throughout the world can however, achieve a much longer lasting happiness.

9. Happiness through humility

Humility is to be self- effacing, to be modest, submissive, unassuming, unostentatious, unpretentious, common, unimportant, ordinary, courteous, respectful, polite, poor or simple.

Today these elements of its definition are often perceived quite negatively. Few people seem to want to live a simple life anymore instead they surround themselves with more and more material things whilst making their lives more complex. People see being submissive or self-effacing as being weak and so many books have been written to help overcome these weaknesses. Respect, politeness and courtesy seem to be a dying value amongst younger generations. Also being unpretentious, common, or ordinary are considered of less value with our seemingly ever-increasing desire to be famous. Perhaps, instead it would worth considering the possibility of happiness that people can gain through living simply or through being polite and self-effacing.

After the Thai Tsunami, I was privileged to go out and help the survivors. When I was there, I was struck by their depth of humility. They had lost everything yet they were more concerned with our well-being, as volunteers, than theirs. Those who had lost loved ones somehow consoled themselves with their belief that they would go on to live a better life. Volunteers had gone out there from all over the world to help these poor survivors and yet they saw that they were not poor but rich in their love for each other. Sometimes I wonder that through consuming ourselves with too many drives, ambitions and desires we forget that we can gain happiness through love, simplicity and very little material wealth. In fact those I have seen who seem to have it all seem rarely happy. In the next few chapters we will be looking further into this.

10. Happiness through compassion

The Dalai Lama says, 'Now I think we must strengthen the genuine force of peace. Real peace – not just mere absence of violence or war. Minimizing hate is like internal disarmament but with it must be external disarmament. Peace must develop on mutual trust.'

The greater the level of calm and peace of mind, the greater is our ability to enjoy a happy, peaceful and joyful life. *'Peace of mind or a calm state of mind is rooted in affection and compassion'* and not external events or material possessions. Even those who are struck by catastrophic events, the Dalai Lama believes, eventually recover to a near normal level of day-to-day happiness. He goes on to say: '

Compassion can be roughly defined in terms of a state of mind that is non-violent, non-harming, and non-aggressive. It is a mental state based on the wish for others to be free of their suffering and is associated with a sense of commitment, responsibility and respect towards others. Without the attitude of compassion, if you are feeling closed, irritated, or indifferent, then you can even be appreciated by your best friend and you just feel uncomfortable'.

Genuine compassion is based on the rationale that all human beings have an innate desire to be happy and to overcome suffering. On the basis of the recognition of this equality and commonality, you develop a sense of affinity and closeness with others. With this as a foundation, you can feel compassion regardless of whether you view the other person as a friend or an enemy. Compassion and altruism has a positive impact on our physical and emotional health. Volunteers report feelings of warmth, calmness, increased energy and even euphoria, as well as enhanced self worth.

Exercise 9 – Meditation for compassion
Dalai Lama's Meditation on Compassion

Begin by visualising a person who is acutely suffering - someone who is in pain or in a very unfortunate situation. Think, perhaps, of children starving in the Sudan, or those people who are being tortured for their politics or suffering due to illness. For the first 3 minutes of the meditation, reflect on that individual's intense suffering. Next try to relate that to yourself, thinking 'That individual has the same capacity for experiencing pain, joy, happiness and suffering that I do'. Then try to allow your natural response to arise – a natural feeling of compassion towards that person and how strongly you wish for that person to be free from that suffering. Resolve, in some way, to help that person become relieved from their suffering. Then meditate in a focused, loving way on how that can be done. Hatred can be the greatest stumbling block to the development of compassion and happiness. If you can learn to develop patience and tolerance towards your enemies, then everything else becomes much easier – your compassion towards others begins to flow naturally. All events and phenomena are dynamic, changing every moment - nothing in this world remains static. At any given moment, therefore, no matter how pleasant or unpleasant your experience may be, it will not last. This is what the Dalai Lama emphasises. The acceptance of change can be an important factor in reducing a large measure of our self-created suffering. We cause our own suffering by refusing to relinquish the past.

5. Making This World Our Hell

'We are each our own devils, and we make this world our hell'. Oscar Wilde

We have so far looked at how we can live, love and be happy. Perhaps this book should end here, as it all seems so simple to attain when written in black and white. Yet for many of us living, loving and being happy is far from simple or reachable. It is difficult enough just to survive the hell around us - the frustrations, the stresses, the resentments, the hurts and the disappointments.

Most of us have been conditioned to expect too much from ourselves and from others and have developed personalities that can make our life hell. To be ever more perfect, to be good and to please others, to be strong, to be in control or to be stress prone and to fill every moment with achievement, busyness and the acquisition of material wealth.

Personalities that can make our life Hell

Being too much of a Perfectionist

'The true perfection of man lies, not in what man has but in what man is' Oscar Wilde

Perfectionists have incredibly high standards for everything - in their careers, their hobbies and their relationships. For the top sportsmen or virtuoso musicians perfection may be their only goal. But for many of us we strive for perfection when it may not even be important. Do you know anyone whose homes must be perfectly clean, perfectly decorated and perfectly furnished; whose children must also be perfectly dressed and perfectly behaved. Similarly, those people's work must be done perfectly, often putting in enormous numbers of hours to ensure that it is so. Even their hobbies and exercise have to be perfect, having personal trainers and running the most number of miles each day in attempts to win marathons. Perfectionists really do feel the need to get things 100% right, no matter what the costs are in terms of stress and fatigue, for fear of the most unbearable response - criticism. Criticism confirms that they might be fallible or human.

Caroline was a perfectionist. That is why those who knew her endearingly thought of her as being able to walk on water. She spent more time than anyone at the office, making sure that everything she did was perfect. If she didn't think her work was quite perfect, she would lie awake at night thinking about it, so instead she would often stay up all night until it was done. She eventually had a mini nervous breakdown and realised she was not superhuman after all.

Adam Phillips, psychologist and author, talks about there being fundamentally two types of person:- the immaculate and the fallible. He says

'For the immaculate everything they do must be right. For them getting it right is the point. For the fallible, 'wrong' is only the word for people who need to be right.'

Getting the right balance between perfection and fallibility, for Caroline was a crucial goal towards achieving physical and psychological well being.

Whist we all strive for perfection at the outset, it might be worth thinking about what would happen if you did something less perfectly. Who would be most disappointed - others or you and how much difference would it make to the outcome? The Pereto principle states that it often takes 20% of your time to do 80% of a job and then it takes 80% of your time to get the other 20% finished perfectly. I'm not saying just do 20%, but maybe finishing that last 20% is not always a life and death matter!

Being Too Good

'I have met hundreds of good women, I never seem to meet any but good women, the world is perfectly packed with good women. To know them is a middle-class education.' Oscar Wilde

As a good, person and a people-pleaser, you are sentenced to saying 'yes' all the time, even when you really want to say 'no'. Your whole existence is about wanting to please. How many times have you heard the phrase, 'But I didn't want to hurt their feelings'? As a pleaser, you could never have the 'call waiting' telephone system, which blips to say there is someone trying to get through when you are on the line, because you could never find a way of interrupting the person you are talking to. Either way you might hurt someone's feelings! Good people and pleasers have a sweet smile on their face, but what is that sweet smile hiding? Could it be a grim resentment for their lack of self-assertion? If you have a suspicion that you may be a pleaser, do you *really* want to spend your life pleasing people rather than fulfilling your own dreams? Do you worry that if you don't please people then they will not like you any more, or that they will criticise or ridicule you for not doing the right thing?

> **Katherine Ward,** *a successful lawyer, was allegedly a good person and a pleaser. She was also considered by her colleagues to be vivacious, wealthy, talented, successful, attractive, warm, kind and generous - but to what cost? Just after Christmas she jumped from the ledge of a London hotel in despair.*

Tim Lott, writer and journalist, tried to understand how a person, like Katherine, could get to this point. He believed that people who felt a strong need to see themselves as 'good' have often done a kind of Devil's bargain in childhood to be good for their parents. But when they never feel quite good enough, a terrible guilt and regret ensues. Tim said that he personally felt guilty that he wasn't ever good enough. He felt a failure because his standards, like those of many young professionals, were always extremely high. He felt unhappy because everyone he knew seemed happy and he was jealous of them. He felt unhappy because he felt unhappy and guilty because he felt guilty. He said it was a terrible downward spiral.

I have a queue of 'Katherines' and 'Carolines', coming to see me to try to understand what is behind their desperate need for perfection. As Dorothy Rowe, author, says they believe that 'if only I were good enough, my parents would start loving me or stop criticising me or failing me". When working with these clients, I suggest to them 'What if you say no?' When asked to do something, I suggest they think:

- 'Do I really want to do this?'
- 'How can I do this?'
- 'Does this person matter enough to me for me to say yes anyway?'
- 'Will their request compromise what really matters to me?'

If you don't want to do this thing or the person doesn't matter or you feel compromised by doing it then I suggest they say 'No'. If, however, the person means so much to you that you feel compelled to say 'yes' then that's OK as long as that person doesn't then persistently ask for more and more from you. Of course this is all easier said than done. Comfortably saying 'No', however, is one of the most difficult things for a 'pleaser' to do, and it takes a great deal of practice. It's a wonderful feeling when you can say 'no' comfortably. It's a feeling of being in control of your life at last. You will find that you have so much more energy for your own pleasures and the things that really matter to *you*.

A song by the Indie band The Killers reminds me of being good. To me being good is like being a puppet or as it is put in the lyrics of the song *Are we human or are we dancer*. This is the chorus:

> Are we human or are we dancer?
> My sign is vital, my hands are cold
> And I'm on my knees looking for the answer
> Are we human or are we dancer?
> Killers

Being Too Strong

The 'strong' of this world can do it all. They have demanding jobs, spend quality time with their children, do their bit around the house and look amazing throughout. They travel the world with their jobs and yet find time to get to the gym. Don't they make you sick? The rest of us are desperately trying to survive yet another crisis! The problem is, the 'strong' of this world, like the perfectionists, are not actually that strong, they are just amazingly self-controlled, adhering to strict, self-imposed schedules and rarely having a moment for themselves. They actively avoid situations in which they might need to ask for help. If they are lost, they will not ask for directions, because it may look like a sign of weakness - instead they take hours trying to find the place for themselves. Just think about a 'strong' person you know. Don't they often have a fixed look on their face, thinking about the next challenge they have to overcome?

Joanne *was one of the strong of this world. She had had a tough childhood. Her parents had divorced when she was only 6 years old and she could only remember them arguing all the time. Even when they split up the rows continued. Her mother had gone out to work after the divorce, and was socialising most nights, so Joanne was left with childminders and babysitters. She laughed it all off, and said that she also had a few friends but spent most of her time absorbed in books, which she devoured. She had learnt from an early age to be totally self-reliant and never to ask for help - a trait which endured until her 38th birthday, when she realised that, despite being successful in her work and social life, she still had not been able to open herself up to an intimate and possibly dependent relationship.*

If you are one of the 'strong' of this world then face it, do you really *want* to be that strong? Do you really want to never ask for help and have to do everything yourself? There are two things that can happen here - either find out why you have to be so damned strong through seeing a therapist, or simply ask for help occasionally. When I say 'simply' it sounds simple, doesn't it? But of course it is the most difficult thing you might have ever done in your life. If you are 'strong', to ask for help might mean being rejected, which is too difficult a thought for you to bear, or it might reveal to others that you have a weakness and are vulnerable. It could also mean that your friends are only too relieved to find out that you are human after all, and that they can do something for you, instead of you always doing something for them. I know, with myself and with others I have spoken to, that friends have often been brought closer by a request for help.

Being Too Controlling

Being too controlling can be a fearsome type of person, because not only are they strong and feel a need to stay in control, but they also try to control everyone else in order to retain their strength. Through this behaviour, they often then alienate themselves from the people they love most. Or they make those people feel unable to take control of their own lives. Controllers tend to have people around them who are more compliant and co-dependent. The world that controlling people inhabit is usually quite fearsome, because they perceive that to let go of their control could cause their world to fall apart. A 'controller' is therefore a difficult person to live with.

__Larna__ came to me admitting that she was quite a controlling sort of person. She came from Africa, where her grandfather had been a strong tribal leader. She had said that, while she loved her partner, George, she also felt the need to control him or, as she put it, 'Larna knew best'. George was a quiet, amenable sort of guy, and generally didn't mind Larna being in charge. It was Larna, however, who felt uncomfortable about their increasingly unequal relationship. She often shouted at him and felt he could never get things right. Through looking at the tribal relationships in Africa, and her own relationship with her father (who was also very dominating), Larna realised that her behaviour was totally inappropriate for today's modern way of living. She had some couple's counselling with George and has since learnt how to respect and love him as an equal, without the need to control every moment of his life. She was then pleasantly surprised at how competent he was!

These are some behaviours I have noted from controlling people:

- Having to be right all the time. Discussions feel like conflicts.
- Having to have everything their way, otherwise they may sulk or not do anything.
- Democracy is not in their vocabulary.

- Leaders who ensure others follow
- Things generally have to be organised and in place.
- The need to organise and control everyone else.
- Rarely see the other person's point of view.
- Rarely seek help from others unless they are ordering them.

When I meet these controllers, however, I wonder if deep down they would actually prefer to be looked after? Maybe they were not looked after enough as a child, or were overwhelmed by similarly controlling parents? It is often helpful, through going to a therapist, to understand the basis of your need for control. Alternatively you could try relinquishing control of some small thing, and see what happens.

Being too Chaotic
I never put off 'til tomorrow what I can possibly do the day after - Oscar Wilde

Being calmly organised is not for the chaotic: it is more a nightmare of stress, procrastination, frustration and guilt. Let's have a look at how chaotic you can be in your day to day life.

Exercise 10 – how chaotic are you?
Tick those that you might say Yes to:

1. **Do you worry needlessly?** Are you almost looking for something to worry about?
2. **Do you suddenly do something risky without even thinking of the consequences?**

3. **Do you have mood swings all within a short period and for no good reason?**
4. **Do you find it difficult to concentrate sometimes?** Are you instead easily distracted, or drift away in the middle of a page or a conversation?
5. **Do you often leave things to the last minute or let them mount up?** As you put off one task, however, you take up another great idea you have had. By the end of the day, week or month you have started many projects, while few have been completed. Do you find, however, there are some days when you can move mountains and be creatively brilliant?
6. **Can you be overly impulsive?** You might enthusiastically say what comes to mind without necessarily considering the appropriateness of your remark. Or, more dangerously, you might impulsively spend money, change plans, career or even relationships. From past mistakes, failures and frustrations you soon learn that it might be easier to keep quiet or do nothing, and feel less confident because of this.
7. **Do you often feel restless?** Could the idea of boredom be so dreadful that you are always on the lookout for something new, exciting and creative to do? Because of this low boredom threshold do you have difficulty following lengthy rules and regulations?

8. **Can you 'tune out' without realizing** if you become angry or frustrated? This might be while reading or watching television, or more seriously through the use of substances such as food, alcohol or drugs, gambling, shopping or overworking?

Pretty much everyone can identify with some of this behaviour, as most of us can be disorganised to some level for some of the time. For women, hormone imbalances can make us more chaotic. For all of us, the increasing stresses of everyday life can lead to more disorganised thinking and more chaotic behaviour. But for the truly chaotic, the answer to most of these questions is 'yes'.

From the 80s onwards companies, through developing a 'Profit is God' approach to business, have consistently increased stresses, year on year, upon their workforce. Their aim was to achieve maximum efficiency for maximum profits, which means demanding increased levels of excellence - perfection, goodness, strength and control from their employees, whilst minimizing chaos and disorder.

As compensation for such excessive work related demands, many people have turned to spending their hard earned money on material comforts, using the latest technology such as High Definition or 3D TVs, the latest laptops and i-pads, i-players and mobile phones that offer music, video, photo albums, television, radio, games and literally millions of other applications. Technology may seem to enhance our lives, but on the flip side we have new breeds of irritants and stressors.

Technophobic chaos
Undoubtedly technology has helped the poorest people of the world help themselves, in terms of better food production and global access to educational materials. Also, we have a vast and immediate source of information at our fingertips and we can buy practically anything we want online, from anywhere in the world, and get it delivered within days. On the downside, however, no longer can we simply phone up a business, council or utility company and ask for a department to help with a particular query, without being faced with highly complex phone diverting systems asking us to choose between options 1 to 6 on several tiers! Having eventually reached a real person, we find we have been diverted to a developing country and are often faced with trying to understand limited English of the person on the other end! Innocent people, especially the elderly, are being taken advantage of by exploitative cold calling or through their computers being hacked into or identities being stolen. How much does all this technology, therefore, simplify, or complicate, our lives?

Organised people, or young people who have been brought up with technology, can make the most of the wonderful tools that today's technology has to offer. They can easily understand all the instructions demanded of them, as well as the complex processes involved when things inevitably go wrong. They can follow all the choices presented to them on the telephone and understand the polite little voices on satellite navigations systems (Sat Nav.), which occasionally command rather ambiguous instructions. For the disabled and the elderly, or simply those who are more chaotic, or not quite as intellectually gifted, these choices and instructions can become a regular nightmare. By the time you get to option 6 on the telephone, many people have forgotten what the earlier options were, not to mention then pressing the wrong button by mistake and having to start over, listening to the data protection monologues all over again. Or having to remember which password you might have for which account or, God forbid, what transactions were made within the last week, when asked. And when things do go wrong, people are often reluctant to sort them out, because the thought of hours on a telephone with services from all over the world is just too much to bear. As for Sat Navs, how many of us have ended up at the farmyard misunderstanding that bear left can just mean follow the road? Or missed a turning, not believing that the Sat Nav. can be sending us down such a small road, not realising that it has been set on shortest route!

*An elderly friend, **Jim**, came to me in utter despair. He had tried to book a short, four day cruise for himself and his wife. As they were both in their mid to late 80s, it was probably the last holiday they would book. He had been under a lot of stress looking after his infirm wife, and persuaded her that the short break would be just what they needed. After working through all the options and data protection statements on the telephone he finally spoke to a nice lady from the travel company. Being hard of hearing, Jim finds the telephone a difficult medium to work with but, despite being a bit of a silver surfer, the computer seemed, for him, a worse option. He had just got to the point of paying, having given all his details to the lady, when she pointed out that he needed insurance in order to go. He was then told that unless he booked the cruise there and then he might lose the offer. The lady said she could call him back to save losing his details. He went off to explore the internet for the best value travel insurance. But, the task became daunting as he found out that very few insurance companies cover people over the age of 85, particularly if they've had heart surgery in the past! Nearly two hours later he had found the best value quote, but had missed the call from the lady who then did not call back.*

Eventually he got back to the travel company, who said he would have to give all his details again as they could not find any record of him. Having done that, Jim was asked if they needed assistance on arrival at the port - if so, they would have to complete a rather long form, which would be sent to them. Finally, just prior to payment, the travel company asked him if he had a passport that was valid for six months, which seemed odd as they were only going to visit places in Europe. Having looked at his own and his wife's passports, he found out that they only had three months to go and would then have to go through what they perceived as the impossible process of re-newing both passports! This was a step too far for him, and he told the nice lady where to go with her holiday. The stress of arranging a pleasurable and stress-free holiday had just become too much.

So why is it that the organised are able to utilise modern technology to simplify their lives and can embrace most challenges put upon them, whilst the chaotic, the less gifted or the elderly seemingly live ever more complicated existences? Organised people manage their time perfectly, never forget people's birthdays and they always remember to write little thank you notes after any event they have been invited to or gifts they have received. Then there are the rest of us, who do our Christmas shopping at the last minute, who forget birthdays, appointments, to return calls or to pay the bills. But then there are the seriously chaotic like Mark.

'Mark couldn't start his day without two cups of coffee and a cigarette. At work a continuous drip feed of coffee got him through until lunch, when he went off to the gym, which he

said was healthier than going to the pub. But he still had to have a quick smoke after. He was very good at his job, which he loved, but he felt he needed to keep 'shaping up' job wise, or his bosses might replace him. So he constantly sought out new successes and achievements. And if that wasn't enough as a hobby, he would do a bungee jump 'for relaxation'. After all that stimulation, Mark needed to get his cigarette and wine fix as well as a stream of multi media systems to relax him on the rare occasions he was at home in the evening. Usually he was out at night and wanted loud music and lots of stimulation. If he was really going for it then he would take cocaine or ecstasy to keep up his confidence and stamina to drink and dance all night with his younger colleagues. He finished off the day, if possible, in bed with a new girl, hoping to have his best orgasm yet, perhaps with a bit of help from his little blue pills. He constantly would hear about how bad all these drugs were for him, but somehow he kept taking them to help him stay on top of his charismatic, creative but chaotic world of drive, disorganisation, distractibility and occasional depression.

Talking with me, Mark realised he had identified with nearly all of the chaotic behaviours, as well being a very hyperactive person. Mark was convinced that he had had a condition called Attention Deficit Disorder (ADD) or ADHD with added Hyperactivity since he was a child. He had always had difficulties at school and had often been in trouble. It was less easy for him, however, to convince his GP, or even the specialists, who sceptically told him that his school behaviour was likely to have been youthful male exuberance.

After completing many questionnaires and tests and speaking to more specialists, it was agreed that he had ADHD. He was then able to replace his illicit cocaine habit with the prescribed and less dangerous stimulant, Ritalin.

Society often writes chaotic people off as either lazy, depressed, anxious or over-excitable, but they can also be very creative and intelligent. In the midst of their disorganization and distractibility, they show flashes of brilliance. Let us take a look at some well-known philosophers, creative writers and musicians. Why do you think many of them took stimulant drugs? A famous self-medicator with the stimulant cocaine was Sigmund Freud, who used it, perhaps, to help him write his multitude of brilliant works. Jean-Paul Sartre wrote his later books while on amphetamines, knowing that he was hastening his death but preferring the short, productive life.

Many modern musicians and other highly creative people profess to have created their best music, lyrics or ideas whilst on drugs. City stock brokers and traders seem to absolutely thrive on risk, stimulation, excitement and pressure. Many, like Mark, take cocaine or other stimulant drugs to help them focus during their extremely demanding working day and then drink too much alcohol or take depressant drugs in the evening to calm back down and to sleep. More recently there have been an increasing number of Ritalin-type, brain-boosting drugs, such as Modalert 200 available which will be discussed in Chapter 6.

Being too Stress Prone
Stress prone people tend to be driven, demanding, ambitious and competitive. People like this can't help but make their world their hell. Take a look at this short questionnaire to check if you may be this type of personality.

Exercise 11 – stress prone

Do you often feel rushed with no time to spare?	yes/no
Are you generally competitive?	yes/no
Are you generally impatient?	yes/no
Do you try to do more than one thing at a time?	yes/no
Do you talk very quickly?	yes/no
Do you give 100% to everything you do?	yes/no
Do you anticipate others and finish their sentence or interrupt?	yes/no
Are you ambitious?	yes/no
Do you eat quickly?	yes/no

If you have more 'yes' than 'no' answers, then it is likely that you are moving towards having a 'stress prone' personality. Psychologists have demonstrated that various illnesses, in particular coronary heart disease, are more prevalent amongst 'stress prone' people. On the other hand easy-going, relaxed, un-rushed and less ambitious people can often achieve as much as stress prone people, but they just go about it in a different way.

Stimulation excites and awakens us to life - Stress can destroy us
Stimulation is what keeps us human beings sharp and at peak performance, but only up to a point.

Our *autonomic nervous system* is our action/recovery centre. When faced with a danger, crisis or stress, our ***action/recovery system*** automatically calls on our **action centre** (*sympathetic nervous system*), to pre-pare us for action, and we experience many bodily changes such as dilated pupils, quicker breath-ing, increased heartbeat, slower digestion and more adrenaline. When the danger has passed, our **recovery/maintenance centre** (*parasympathet-ic nervous system*), facilitates relaxation, recovery and maintenance of our body through increased salivation, slower heartbeat and breathing and stim-ulated digestion.

Humans today, however, with our amazingly devel-oped brain, are able to defer such immediate survival responses to stimuli. For example we would not, if we were psychologically threatened or bullied necessarily respond by fighting or by running away. We have to weigh up legal and cultural implications of taboos on violence or fighting as well as the benefits of deferring any direct actions in favour of following more acceptable indirect protocols.   Added to this we often defer rests following persistent stress, in favour of achieving longer-term goals. The problem is that man's simplest 'fight-or-flight' part of the brain is still designed for cave men, so too much stimulation can lead to stress chemicals which have been produced not being used up, which can cause us to feel exhausted, tense and irritable.

Continuous, long-term stress, without sufficient rests and relaxation, can, therefore, lead to heart and circulatory diseases, ulcers, infectious diseases, skin diseases and even, in extreme cases, death.

What are today's stresses?
There are many stresses in this highly sophisticated, demanding and technological world that we either create for ourselves (internal stresses) or those that we are surrounded by i.e. external stresses. Internal stressors are those relating to our personality ie how much we perceive the world as being stressful, whilst external stressors are those that occur around us e.g. noise, discrimination, work, financial strain, marriage and children. Or stress can occur through

an extreme incident, such as a road traffic accident, a violent attack or a near death experience.

Internal Stresses

Internal stresses are those relating to how we perceive life i.e. whether we perceive it to be stressful or not. These are often linked to our personalities as we have discussed already.

External Stresses

External Stresses can occur both within our personal lives or work based or it can come from extreme incidents we may experience such as a road traffic accident or a violent attack.

Personal stresses - are what we face in our personal lives. These include:

- *Communications breakdowns:* it is so easy for communication between couples to deteriorate which can cause frustration and stress
- *Giving birth/moving house:* both often happen at the same time, doubling the stress
- *Being financially challenged:* nobody wants to be in debt, but it can happen to anyone due to redundancy, sickness, pregnancy/children, divorce or over-spending
- *Sexual problems:* sex both keeps a relationship together and splits it. Sexual frustration is stressful and upsetting

- *Separation/divorce:* this usually a stressful and emotional time for the whole family
- *Death, illness or caring for another:* bereavement, serious illness or caring for someone close to us can be an extremely upsetting and stressful personal crisis. Grieving is an important part of coming to terms with loss. It can, however, be difficult to know how to cope from day to day, and the first few months can be extremely stressful.

Work stresses - In your job, you may be finding it difficult to meet deadlines; you may feel frustrated at bad communication with co-workers; the commute may be difficult and exhausting; or there may be personality clashes among your colleagues. Other work stressors are:

- *Organisational change:* cutbacks, cultural or technological changes or major organisational rationalisation.
- *Relationships at work:* lack of support, hierarchical status, personality clashes or rivalries, intimate affairs.
- *Bullying and harassment:* this can happen due to race, gender, religion, disability, culture, social class, appearance or regional accent. Or through verbal, physical or group bullying which can cause victims to feel isolated, stressed and deeply upset.

- ***Diminishing staff morale:*** due to cutbacks, lack of trust and bad management.
- ***Work factors:*** too much work; work that is too difficult; too little work; undemanding work; role ambiguity; role conflict; too much responsibility; job insecurity and fear of redundancy; noise; heat; overcrowding; unsociable shifts; long hours.

Extreme Crisis Stresses - such as road, rail or air accidents; robberies or raids; terrorist attacks; muggings; rape; sudden deaths; suicides and extreme verbal or physical assaults. These can be experienced on four different levels: Direct experience of either being involved in or witnessing the incident; being a relative or friend of a victim; helping to manage the experience; or being involved as a community with the incident. The effects are often enough to temporarily emotionally overwhelm those involved, meaning they almost immediately feel unable to cope with their daily life.

How stress imbalances our body and mind

At a physiological level, the effect of stresses is that of stimulation, awakening a pattern of stress responses designed to prepare the individual for 'fright', 'fight' or 'flight'. Unfortunately, many stresses in today's civilised world permit neither a fight nor a flight response, nor are they generally resolved in the short-term. Running from an uncomfortable meeting, attacking your boss or hiding behind underneath your desk are not helpful or productive solutions. Thus, if the source of stress continues, and heightened readiness for defence persists, then gradually the body can be damaged, sometimes leading to irreversible harm to organs such as the heart and major arteries.

Neil had been working on a long term and very demanding project. He worked long hours in his international IT support role. He loved his job and wouldn't dream of letting his colleagues down. He had a wife and young children at home, and being relatively new to the country was also finding his personal life quite stressful. He normally dealt with stress very well, which is why he was so successful at his job - but this project had gone on for much longer than his normal projects and the pressure had been mounting up. Having been promoted, he had also wanted to take on other responsibilities. He knew that he was stressed and had not been sleeping very well. He admitted to himself that he smoked too much and had put on a lot of weight recently, but felt confident that he could manage everything. He had not been feeling well but had wisely planned a holiday to have a break and attend to his health. Unfortunately, just prior to that holiday, he suffered a severe heart attack at work and died, tragically, in front of his colleagues.

The negative psychological effects of prolonged stress involve the disruption of intellectual, emotional and behavioural functions.

Exercise 12 – effects of stress

Tick those that you may identify with.

Physiological effects of stress

Stress hormones in the blood
Raised heart rate/BP/ Respiration
Raised blood sugar levels
Increased body metabolism
Increased muscle tension
Heightened sensory aware- ness
Digestive system slowing/ breakdown

Psychological effects of stress

Impairment of attention
Concentration problems
Perceptual distortions
Memory failures
Unrealistic thinking
Reduced problem-solving ability

Emotional effects of stress

Raised anxiety
Depression
Loss of interest
Self blame
Sudden temper outbursts

Behavioural effects of stress

Loss of energy
Loss of focus & Goals
Altered sleep patterns
Reduced ability to make decisions
Lower performance

Stress effects of an extreme crisis

In the first few days

Shock, which can include numbness, distress, disbelief and a feeling of being generally overwhelmed and un- able to cope.

During the next few weeks, reactions include:
- Re-experiencing the event or avoiding associations to it
- Sleeping problems, nightmares
- Lack of concentration
- Anxiety or being easily startled
- Withdrawal and/or relationship difficulties
- Back ache, headaches, tension, panic or exhaustion

Nb Post Traumatic Stress Disorder (PTSD) is the definition for prolonged posttraumatic stress reactions (beyond 4 weeks). It may develop into the following conditions: depression, raised blood pressure, lower immune system or long term illness.

Or just being too female? The Hormonal hell

"Women, the old argument goes, are eternally subject to the whims and wherefores of their biological clocks. Their raging hormonal cycles make them emotionally unstable and intellectually unreliable. If women have second-class status, we are told, it is because they cannot control the implacable demands of that bouncing estrogen' (Karen Paige, 1973)

I was at a party recently where my girlfriends were talking about their various ailments. Pat said she gets angry and irritable at a certain time every month, which results in making her kids and her husband lives hell. Caroline, who had just given birth, said that she had felt miserable ever since. As if her whole personality had changed since her son was born. Susan, was complaining of constant hot flushes, tiredness and her roller coaster emotions since hitting 40. Then Paula told everyone about the horrendous battle she had had with her doctor trying to get a true diagnosis of why she had piled on loads of weight and become extremely exhausted over the previous six months.

But what was this all about?

Premenstrual Syndrome 'Don't Blame me its PMT'
Pat had been suffering from Premenstrual Syndrome (PMS), a disorder which happens to as many as one in three women all over the world. There is a complex fluctuation of estrogen and progesterone hormones every month, just prior to bleeding, which causes symptoms of this disorder. These symptoms are irritability, low confidence, low energy levels, breast tenderness, food cravings particularly for sweet things and abdominal bloatedness. They arrive regularly every month and can lead to feelings of resentment from family, colleagues and friends.

Postnatal depression 'Baby Blues'
It sounded like Caroline may have been experiencing postnatal depression (PND), which affects 10% of new mothers after their baby's birth and can be

extremely debilitating. Most women get what is called 'baby blues' about 3 days after birth due to large fluctuations in estrogen and progesterone. But for the unfortunate ones, like Caroline, it didn't end. Women describe postnatal depression as feeling distant, shattered, confused, out of control, angry and panicky. As with most depression there are risks associated with the guilt, the lowering of self-esteem and the general reduction in concentration and ability. A cocktail that has often led to suicide.

Menopause

Susan was likely to have been suffering from the menopause. Whilst the menopause signifies the end of estrogen reproduction, the peri-menopause is when the hormones start winding down. Throughout this whole period there are fluctuations of hormones, the number of days of the menstrual cycle and the amount of blood flow. A woman may feel emotional imbalances as in PMS but these are not confined to just the days before bleeding, they may go on for months and months. There can also be symptoms of hot flushes, tiredness and insomnia. The menopause can cause weight gain, vaginal drying, incontinence, bone loss and heart problems It is all around this time, because of estrogen loss, that the vagina becomes smaller and drier; the urinary tract also becomes thinner and drier with involuntary losses of urine; the skin becomes less elastic and dryer leading to more wrinkles; hair may become dry and thin; gums recede and bleed; weight increases by approximately 10 pounds; bone loss increases and the cardiovascular system is less efficient.

Hypothyroidism

Paula was finally diagnosed with hypothyroidism. The thyroid gland is an important organ of the endocrine system. It is located in the front of the neck just below the voice box. The gland produces the hormone thyroxine, which controls the way every cell in the body uses energy. This process is called metabolism. When there isn't enough thyroxine, the body slows down and most people then put on weight and feel exhausted (hypothyroidism or under active thyroid). Despite one in fifty women suffering from it in Britain and 10% of women 45-54, having it, the UK has wider normal ranges for the condition than the rest of Europe and America. This means that, if you are on the borderline of having hypothyroidism your condition is likely to be ignored by GPs, with the presumption of being just FFFF (GP speak for fat, female, fatigued and forty) or worse stressed or depressed.

We will be looking at how we can escape our hell in chapter 7.

6. Fragility of Man

I was called to attend the scene of a suicide involving a leap from the top of a magnificent marble, deco style staircase. As I looked down from the sixth floor, which was from where the man jumped, a beautiful crystal chandelier was dripping from the ceiling, down through the well, towards the bottom at basement floor level. I then pictured, from witness accounts, how this unfortunate person might have looked, seconds after he had jumped to his death; limp and surrounded by a large pool of blood, lying amongst the shattered shards of glass. He had certainly ended his life dramatically, taking with him, most of the chandelier and witnessed by an audience of horrified shoppers. This tragic suicide powerfully illustrates just how precarious and fragile human beings are. We are simply a fragile network of flesh, bones, nerves, cells, enzymes, blood and water. And yet our structure is so complex that we still, in this highly advanced society, don't fully understand it.

Sam went off on a charity cycle ride through Cambodia. He had trained for months and researched all the precautions necessary for a ride in such hot conditions. He had also had regular yearly medical checks, so despite being in his mid-50s he was confident that all would go well. And all did go well until, due to the extreme heat during that week, he suddenly became very thirsty and tired. He thought he was drinking isotonic (mineral supplemented) water and continued to quench his seemingly endless thirst. On that day, however, inexplicably, the mineral supplements had been left out or were depleted, which meant as Sam drank he was not receiving the salt replacement that he so badly needed. He became dangerously ill with a condition that amounts to drowning in your own body (Hyponatremia), where body cells fill up with excess water and the vital organs then begin to close down. He became very sick but thanks to the quick response of the team doctor and his colleagues taking him on a seemingly impossible journey across rivers and difficult terrain and reviving him when he was nearly dying, he finally got to a hospital in time for his life to be saved, although he was in intensive care on life support for many days, whilst it was uncertain whether his organs would ever recover.

Sports people like those we have already mentioned such as Beckham, Tiger Woods and Roger Federer also respect how fragile their human bodies are and have regular medical checks as well as researching what extreme situations could be potentially dangerous for them. Living a healthy life doesn't, however, mean having to live a boring life. In fact, it usually means living a more active, vibrant and interesting life, albeit with a full understanding of the needs of your mind and body in terms of nutrition, physical fitness and mental health, which we will look at more throughout this book.

Each of us are born with an amazing and highly complex body. Like any vehicle, if we run it and fuel it well then, for most of us, we can rely on having a long and healthy life. Yet many of us don't look after ourselves as well as we look after our cars.

Cars in the UK, legally, need an annual MOT after getting to three years old, yet humans don't have any such regulations. We give our cars regular services, whether or not they are functioning well, yet we do not offer ourselves such care. When our cars don't run smoothly we rarely ignore the problem until the point that it breaks down, yet many of us seem to take this approach to our bodies. We know that our car will not perform as well if we have put the wrong fuel in, or have not added enough oil to the engine, or if we have not recently given it a good run. Yet we put unhealthy junk food and poisons such as alcohol or drugs into our bodies instead of hydrating them, we rarely go for a good run, and still expect to function well.

Clive loved going out and having fun. He had great optimism and if anything went wrong he felt it would just sort itself out. He had, however, been having niggling pains over the last six months in his abdomen but chose to ignore them in favour of another night out and plenty of alcohol which dulled the pain. Unfortunately one night, despite being urged to go to a doctor by his friends his appendix burst and he was lucky to live.

Robert, was also lucky to live. He was in his mid 50s and loved his life. He had retired early and had enjoyed travelling the world with his wife on the large cruise ships. He loved food and alcohol and hated exercise and gardening. He boasted that he had never needed to go to the gym as he felt that he had always lived an active life and had never really been too overweight. What he didn't realise was that a lot of his activity had happened whilst at work. Now retired he, preferred to read the daily papers, have a bit lunch and have a nap in afternoon. He then settled down to a large evening meal a bottle of wine and the television. Over the next couple of years he gradually became less and less active and put on more and more weight. Then one day he felt quite unwell and had a heart attack. Fortunately for him, this wasn't fatal and with modern technology he was able to have a simple procedure to widen his arteries, which were clogged with cholesterol. After such a close shave he realised that he would have to immediately start taking more care of his body. But first he wanted to understand how he got to such a grave situation through finding out how his body worked and also find out what his body needed to stay healthy.

It was interesting, that when I talked to him, he said that he would never dream of running his precious car, without having read its manual in order to get the best efficiency out of it. Yet he had never considered reading a manual about his own body?

I gave him what I had compiled as a beginners manual for human beings which I think is the minimal knowledge essential for the healthy running of our own bodies and minds. This is the science bit, and needs your full attention – but hopefully it will be worth it! If you really feel you don't need a manual or think you know it all then feel free to skip to the next chapter.

Our Amazing Human Brain
The primitive human brain

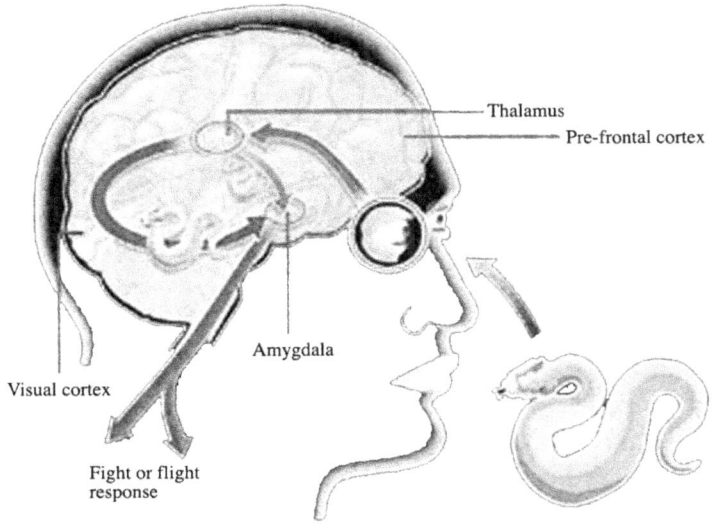

Our human brain is truly amazing. It has evolved, through millions of years, to whatever circumstances were needed at the time. Smell was human's first primal sense, and was vital for survival. Our primitive brain took in what it smelled and sorted it out as to whether it was edible, toxic, sexually available or dangerous. It then sent reflexive messages throughout our body, telling us whether to bite, spit, approach, flee or chase. This was our most basic **autonomic action centre,** functioning to give automatic fight, fright or flight reactions as a response to danger.

Human brains then evolved into something amazing

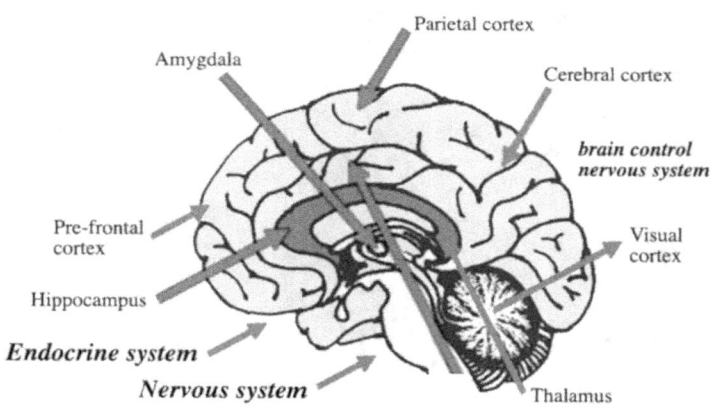

As our primitive brain developed so it grew a *limbic ring* that added our emotions of fury, love, terror or desire. It also refined our learning and memory, which enabled us, as humans to become smarter than other animals in our choices for survival.

We developed two almond shaped tissues (*amygdalas*), one either side of our brain, much larger than other animals, including those of our closest relatives, the primates. These *amygdalas* contribute to our alarm system, which triggers the secretion of our body's 'flight or fight' hormones, adrenaline and cortisol and mobilizes movement; it automatically increases our alertness through the release of *alert energy messengers (noradrenaline).* Added to this it sends a signal for a fearful expression and freezes unrelated movements, such as appetite, sexual desire and other distracting elements. Simultaneously, *cortical memory systems* retrieve any memorised knowledge relevant to overcoming the emergency. It had been found that we have, in fact, two types of memory: our emotional memory, which is related to our amygdalas and our normal memory, including our short and long term memory, which is related to our frontal cortex. When there is an emergency/ trauma, which triggers raised levels of adrenaline/ cortisol, within us, then our memory of that trauma is caught up in our emotional memory, and is less related to verbal/cognitive cues but more to sensory cues such as taste, sight, sound, touch and smell. Unlike our normal memory, this memory has an involuntary recall causing us to have intrusive snapshot type flashbacks. We can then feel overwhelmed by our senses and emotions rather than feel in control. These, put together, are common Post Traumatic Stress reactions, which if prolonged can become Post Traumatic Stress Disorder. Until we can identify our cognitive/verbal associations around the traumatic event, normally through talking about it, then our emotional memory cannot be converted into our normal memory and so be processed into our normal voluntary long term memory.

Humans now have the least stereotyped, most intellectual and most flexible lifestyle of all animal species, and it is believed that our brain *cortex* must be in some way responsible. Flattening out a brain *cortex*, the rat's is the size of a postage stamp, the chimp's is A4 size, while the human has a cortex four times that size.

Our brain *cortex* is the seat of our thoughts: it contains the centres that comprehend what our senses perceive. These are our:

- *motor cortex* for movement of our muscles
- *visual cortex* for seeing
- *auditory cortex* for hearing
- *somatosensory cortex* for touching

Our **planning cortex** (*prefrontal cortex*), further allows us to have feelings about ideas, art, symbols and imaginings; the ability to strategise and plan for the long term; and is responsible for our working memory and emotional reactions, which is what really puts us way beyond all other animals in terms of intellect.

Most sensory information is coordinated by our *planning cortex.* If an emotional response is called for, our **planning cortex** dictates it, working hand in hand with other circuits in our brain. An emotional trigger will cause our **planning cortex** to perform a risk/benefit ratio of our many possible reactions. For animals this is when to either attack or run, but for us humans there are other reactions such as when to placate, persuade, seek sympathy, stonewall or provoke guilt, to name but a few. If our planning cortex connections are severed (as in the 1940's prefrontal lobotomy cure for mental illness) all emotional life falls away.

Our Brain as the Central Headquarters (CHQ) to our Body

Our CHQ, via *neurons*, processes and transmits information to our bodies

Within our brain there are about 100 billion *neurons,* which are nerve cells that process and command and transmit information, both chemically and electronically to our bodies. This is done via messengers called *mood messengers (neurotransmitters/neuromodulators),* which travel along our spinal cord and through to our various *nervous systems.*

Our *peripheral nervous system* functions muscle responses via our *skeletal nervous system* and functions action/recovery responses via our action system (*autonomic nervous system).* Our *endocrine system* functions hormones for growth, strength, metabolism, digestion, stress and sex.

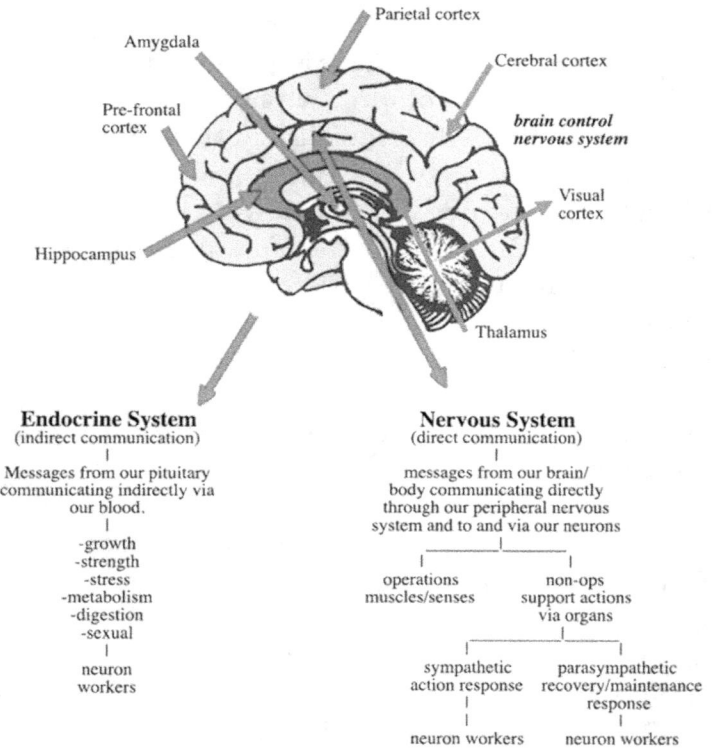

I know this may just be a science a bit too far, but read on if you can – it's worth it to really understand ourselves and how to optimise our health, moods and energy levels. The balance of *mood messengers* relates directly to our happiness, pain, pleasure, emotions, anxiety, appetite, memory, sleep, alertness, stress, depression and general health.

Mood messengers that help us feel good

Mood messenger
Happy messenger
(Serotonin)

mood message
calmness, happiness,
resilience

Higher levels of Serotonin within our body seems to enhance our sense of security and our courage, assertiveness, self-worth, calm, flexibility and resilience. Deficiency in Serotonin has been linked to bad moods and psychological disorders such as depression and anxiety. Exactly what role serotonin plays in the body, and whether it acts independently or with other neurotransmitters, is still not fully clear.

Mood messenger
Alert messenger
(Noradrenaline)
Dopamine

mood message
alertness, focus,
memory, energy

Noradrenaline (known as adrenaline to most of us) is involved with our learning, memory and arousal. Adrenaline deficiency has been linked with Attention Deficit Disorder (ADD), a disorder, which limits attention span and short term memory.

Dopamine is primarily an inhibitory neurotransmitter and is involved in our voluntary movements, learning, memory and arousal. Deficiencies have been linked to Parkinson's disease, a disorder in which the sufferer progressively loses muscle control and with schizophrenia, a disorder of emotion and thought. More recently a dopamine deficiency has also been linked with ADD.

Mood messenger	**mood message**
Buzz messenger	euphoria,
(Endorphins)	reduced pain

Endorphins were discovered from research into the effects of the pain-killing chemical morphine (which comes from the opium poppy). It was believed, from this research, that our body produces its own internal, endogenous, morphine-like substance, hence the term endorphins. Endorphins being inhibitory, once locked into a receptor site do not allow mood messengers, such as those connected with pain, from occupying the same receptor site. Like morphine, therefore, endorphins relieve pain.

Chocolate stimulates all our feel good mood messengers

Chocolate is probably the world's most loved confectionary and the reason why it is so popular, apart from its fabulous taste, is its unique combination of foods - fat, sugar, protein and the magic ingredient - the sticky chocolate liquor, which comes from the cocao bean - that instantly increase nearly all our feel good mood messengers. Chocolate was brought over to Europe in the 17th century, by the Spaniards, who learned its use from the Aztecs at the beginning of the 16th century. Sugar, which chocolate contains, is a carbohydrate with a high glycaemic value (HGV) and therefore has the ability to bring on pleasurable 'high' feelings much quicker than other carbohydrates.

Sara just couldn't have enough of it. She said that she loves chocolate more than she loves sex because it is readily available and has none of the complications of involving other people!!

She eats it for the pure enjoyment of its magical taste, which she loves and to which she has become addicted. But she also eats it when she feels depressed or stressed because it seems to make her feel so much better.

How we can feel good through being in love and being optimistic, positive, excited and active

It has been proved that the happier and more optimistic, positive, *supported* or in love we are, the higher our levels of Serotonin become. Excitement and stimulation can create Alert messengers such as Noradrenaline and rigorous exercise or sex can produce Endorphins.

Sex is probably the world's most loved activity, besides eating chocolate, even though it can create a lot of anxiety as to how it should or should not be done!! As well as sharing intimate contact with our partner, an orgasm sets off those amazing buzzy endorphins. This in turn balances our hormones, releases our tension, and speeds up our heart rate and metabolism. Sex uses up energy and helps burn fat - and it is spontaneous and fun. When we are asked which pastime we enjoy most, sex comes up every time - at least until later middle age. It has been suggested that the release of endorphins occurs as a response to painful and exciting stimuli, and serves to reduce that pain. Endorphin molecules stimulate opiate receptors on some of the neurons in our brain. One consequence of this is an intensely pleasurable effect, just like that reported by heroin users.

Excitement can produce both alert energy (adrenaline) and buzz energy (endorphins) messengers. There can be the excitement of watching or listening to pop or Rock 'n' Roll music or of entering a competition or meeting new people or doing something risky like fast driving, skiing or parachute jumping.

Labour pain and other pains, strenuous exercise and starvation produces endorphins - endorphin levels increase during labour, causing an euphoria in patients. When pain has been experienced in other ways, such as self-mutilation, a type of euphoria is also experienced, probably due to a release of endorphins. Many athletes have reported the euphoric effects resulting from prolonged or strenuous exercise. When we have felt extremely hungry, we again feel euphoric from the rush of endorphins.

None of these ways of gaining our feel good factor messengers are necessarily immediate quickfixes so many people reach for a quick fix route through food or drugs.

How we create calmness, happiness and resilience mood messengers (Serotonin) through food and drugs

Simple HGV carbohydrates produce a rush of the 'happy' messenger, Serotonin. As we have briefly mentioned already in chapter 4 these include all forms of sugar, honey, syrups, alcohol, potatoes, corn and refined foods such as white flour and white rice - more commonly known as junk food or what I call 'couch potato' carbohydrates. In a nutshell, during our digestive process these food carbohydrates enter our blood stream as glucose. The glucose is then broken down by insulin secretion into energy, carbon dioxide, water and an amino acid called Tryptophan. Tryptophan then passes to our brain and combines with vitamin B6 to become the 'happy, calm, resilient' messenger, serotonin. 'Couch Potato' carbohydrates short-cut our body's normal digestive processes, causing glucose to rush straight into our blood stream. This causes us to have an immediate boost of energy and happiness.

The problem is with 'Couch Potato' carbohydrates is that they work on a roller coaster basis with fast 'highs' and similarly fast 'lows' following. So as people feel suddenly low in energy and mood then they reach again for their next fix. Chocolate contains these rapid release carbohydrates, which is probably why so many people become chocoholics. So too can people become addicted to Couch potato carbohydrates, particularly sugar, potatoes and alcohol!

'Runner bean' LGV carbohydrates *Wholewheat/wholegrain products, vegetables and fruit.*

'Runner Bean' carbohydrates are only partly absorbed by our body and produce a smaller, but more lasting amount of energy and happiness. There is not, therefore, the roller coaster effect and so not so much craving for these type of carbohydrates.

Prescription drugs such as the anti-depressant SSRI (Selective Serotonin Re-uptake Inhibitor) drugs can decrease the rate of serotonin re-uptake with relatively few negative side effects. The amount of Serotonin in our system therefore increases which increases our happiness, calmness and resilience. One of the first SSRIs and certainly one of the most talked about anti-depressant was Prozac, but there are now countless others which can be prescribed to suit the individual. Many of my clients who come to me feeling extremely depressed are recommended by their doctors to take SSRIs for a few months. I believe that these can be used well in order to temporarily help increase their mood and resilience whilst also looking at the source of their depression and what they can do to feel back in control of their lives.

Recreational drugs such as Ecstasy and Cannabis causes Serotonin to be released into our brain, making us feel calm, relaxed and happy.

Ecstasy creates warm and loving feelings and an overwhelming desire to dance, which can last for up to ten hours. Self-confidence is increased and sexual confidence is gained. Large amounts of Ecstasy, however, can trigger hallucinations. It causes a rise in blood pressure and sweating and can damage certain brain cells, and if used for a long time could cause liver damage. Over-exertion, usually through hours of dancing, can lead to heatstroke, dehydration, coma, blood clotting and death. Ecstasy can affect body co-ordination, making it dangerous to do things like driving and once the effects wear off, it can leave us feeling miserable. Taken in larger amounts, Ecstasy can cause feelings of anxiety or confusion, even paranoia.

Cannabis, in small amounts, produces a mild, pleasurable 'high', consisting of relaxation, a loss of social inhibition, intoxication, and humour. Speech becomes slurred and co-ordination is impaired much like other depressants such as alcohol. Other effects include increased heart rate, lack of concentration and enhanced appetite (the 'munchies'). Larger amounts, however, result in hallucinogenic reactions such as the perceived slowing of time and amplified sensitivity to colours, sounds, tastes, and smells. As well as increased awareness of bodily states, sexual sensations are also heightened. The habitual use of marijuana often results in extreme paranoia.

How we create alertness, focus, memory and energy mood messenger (Noradrenaline) from *food and drugs*

Protein foods include meat, fish, cheese, eggs, milk, soya, almonds, hazelnuts and certain pulses, lentils, peas and beans if eaten in conjunction with wholegrain. Proteins are made up of chains of amino acids, which enter our blood stream. Brain Tyrosine amino acid is converted to dopamine in our brain with the aid of vitamin B6. Dopamine is then converted to alert energy messenger, with the help of vitamin C. Proteins also keep us feeling fuller for longer if lean and eaten moderately and can help reduce weight.

Prescribed stimulant drugs such as Amphetamines and Ritalin
Amphetamines were first manufactured in the 1930's for treatment of colds and hay fever. They were later found to affect the nervous system, increasing energy, alertness and self-confidence. As a result, they were used extensively by the military in World War Two. Amphetamines were also found to suppress appetite, and were used as 'slimming pills', in the 50's, being freely marketed under such trade names

as Methedrine, Dexedrine and Benzedrine. However, because of their psychological side effects, they were widely abused and can only now be prescribed by a doctor.

Ritalin has been a widely used prescribed drug for improving behaviour in hyperactive children with low attention span. This condition is called Attention Deficit Hyperactivity Disorder (ADHD). Ritalin creates more 'alert energy ' mood messengers, which are deficient in these children and which paradoxically calms their hyperactivity, I have had a number of clients come to me who have been concerned about their children's excessively hyperactive behaviour and low attention span, which was causing them to have a lot of problems at school. Whilst most children can overcome hyperactivity through learning new behaviours, for some if they are diagnosed with ADHD, the only option is to take these Ritalin type drugs, which lower their hyperactivity and increase their attention span and ability to focus. They are then better able to concentrate on their studies as well as learn behaviours that will eventually help them overcome their ADHD without the need for drugs.

Recreational stimulant drugs such as coffee, cigarettes and cocaine
Coffee is a mild stimulant, which increases our 'alert energy' messenger and so increases our focus and energy. Too much of it, however, can cause us to be irritable and nervous.

Cigarettes contain the stimulant nicotine, which creates the 'alert energy' chemical. The downside of smoking, however, is the high possibility of addiction and the many smoking related illnesses including heart disease and lung cancer, which can lead to an early death.

Cocaine is used for a variety of reasons. For many, it serves to increase focus, energy and confidence, so allowing the user to remain alert and energised for many hours, over and above their normal abilities. For ADD sufferers it may, like Ritalin, paradoxically calm their hyperactivity whilst increasing their focus. Too high a dose can, however, seem like being constantly stressed and cause feelings of anxiety and irritability.

Modalert 200 - an increasing number of legal Ritalin-type brain boosting drugs like Modalert 200 (originally designed to treat narcolepsy), which David Aaronovich experienced and talked about in the Times:

> Having taken two Modalert 200 tablets, he felt as if his attention was fixed. This resulted in his meeting going well, his shopping expedition being less fraught and his exercise machine input going considerably up. Aaronovich was sceptical about it's untested long term use.

How we create euphoria enhancing and pain reducing mood *messengers* (endorphins) through drugs

Prescribed drugs such as morphine
As we have seen, morphine has been the basis for pain killers used in medicine. Due to their addictive nature, they are used mainly for terminally ill patients or those with chronic excessive pain.

Recreational drugs – heroin and its associated drugs
Many people are resorting to the modern way of alleviating the pains of today's tribulations by taking heroin, which creates a massive surge of endorphins, thus increasing euphoria and reducing pain. Again there is a problem of addiction and many other downsides of taking such a drug.

7. Escaping our Hell

> 'There are no mistakes in life: only lessons. There is no such thing as a negative experience just opportunities to grow, learn and advance along the road to self-mastery. From struggle comes strength. Even pain can be a wonderful teacher' The Monk Who Sold His Ferrari – Robin Sharma

So now the difficult bit is how we can actually escape our hell and feel free to dare to live, love and be happy. I believe it is about being able to attain balance and about knowing what things are most important to you, then spending your time on these rather than the trivia of life.

Crisis can awaken us to the nature and value of our lifestyles

We have seen that crisis can awaken us to the value of living life. So too can crisis awaken us to what our lifestyle is REALLY like and to the value of getting our lifestyle as we want it.

__Anthony__ was a survivor of a pleasure boat tragedy in the Middle East in 2006. He was having a celebratory night out when the boat he was on capsized. As an engineer, Anthony had always been concerned with balance, but not necessarily his own life balance. He had been one of the lucky ones who had stayed on the top deck of that boat so when it capsized he had been thrown clear into the water. He had saved himself and others from drowning, but many of his friends and work colleagues had died, trapped in the lower deck of the boat. He had since also been haunted by the thought, __"If I had died on that night I may never have played with my children."__ Anthony admitted that, due to so many work projects with tight deadlines, he was at the office for far too many hours of the day and then could not relax at home or sleep very well at night. He even admitted that he rarely laughed or played with his family and was generally too serious a person. His father, a teacher, had been very strict with Anthony as a child. He had often beaten him and always said "don't rather than "do". His older brother had died as a baby and as a result of this, from the moment Anthony was born, his father had been far too over-protective of him and had not really allowed him to be a free child. Anthony felt very sad when he realised that this overprotection had left him, as an adult, feeling unable to play with his children. Instead, like his father, he was being too strict with them.

I commented that perhaps he could now choose for himself how he wanted to be with his children. That he could play with them more and be a little less strict. In doing this Anthony also then had a second chance to develop and free his own inner child. Anthony came back to me after the weekend to tell me how happy he felt that he had been able to play with his children and laugh with his wife. He still had a heavy sense of responsibility and duty, which he said he was working on and agreed that he wanted to follow the rule that I had mentioned to him - that only 5% of his day to day experience should be dealing with the past, 15% of his day should be spent planning for the future and the other 80% should be spent living and enjoying the present - to enjoy being as well as doing.

Anthony's case reminded me of another young lad, Tom, who had tragically died within an incredibly busy IT company.

Tom was an employee of a small IT company, which was rapidly growing. All the employees felt they had to work long hours and most weekends in order to meet their growing deadlines. The work atmosphere had become heavy and too serious with most employees having their heads down into their computers most of the time. Yet Tom's colleagues told me that his presence always made their lives lighter through seeing his smile and hearing his little stories and jokes. One said 'He always had time to check out how we were and remembered important information about our lives'. Tom connected to each and every one of them and made their dedicated but rather serious lives more enjoyable. They commented sadly on how much they would miss him and I asked them perhaps what they had learnt from him. They said that they had learnt that despite intense pressure of work and tight deadlines they would still make time for lighter chat and concern for each other.

After the 9/11 bombings, which involved so many 'high flying' professionals, a large number of them went to see therapists, both in the UK and the States, trying to understand why they had devoted so much time to working and so little time to living. 'We just don't have a life balance', many said. Then, the UK had its own 7/7 London Underground and bus bombings. On both occasions I worked with many of the successful city survivors, who wanted to seriously reassess their lives in the light of what they had experienced, in order to get a better life balance.

Crisis forces us to think about what is really important.

Tragedies can therefore prompt us to look at our lives clearly, perhaps even for the first time. I see so many clients who, for many reasons, have lost the balance between their work and personal lives. They come to me complaining of stress and want me to help them develop a stress resilience. When I ask them to look honestly at their lives, they usually recognise an outrageously negative imbalance of lifestyle. Their work has often completely taken over their lives – body and soul. Just like that pleasure boat, they are close to capsizing.

__Jennifer__ came to me from one of the top management and financial consulting firms. She was what I call a typical recruit for these places: a perfectionist, an inherently good people-pleaser, an incredibly hard worker, socially unskilled and lacking in the ability to say 'No'. Her work therefore 'suited' her perfectly and she became one of their top consultants. She worked away from home a lot and when at a client's office, the whole team would usually stay until two or three in the morning. Whilst most of her colleagues would make sure that they took good breaks throughout the night, she would prefer to crack on until she had got the job right. She would then slump into bed exhausted, having quickly consumed a room service burger and chips. And that had been her life for the last 5 years. She was depressed because she was overweight and did not have time to exercise. She said she knew what was healthy to eat and how to keep fit but she just did not have any time to do it. Her company had provided stress management seminars, so she knew all about that too. But she was just too tired to follow their advice.

I helped Jennifer look at her lifestyle and find out what it was that kept her working such long hours rather than saying 'No' to these demands. She realised that perfectionism and pleasing others was what validated her self-esteem. Socialising involved possible rejection, especially as she felt fat and ugly, so it was safer for her not to bother. She was stuck in a rut of work/life imbalance that had led her to depression and general ill health. After much soul searching, Jennifer tried practising newly learned assertiveness skills. But she still found it very difficult to say 'No' to her over-demanding bosses. Instead, she changed her job to work for a government agency where her talents were more appreciated and the demands were not anywhere near as inhuman. She then had more time and energy to work on her eating/body/mind fitness. She told me recently that she no longer feels that she has to comfort eat, as she is not so exhausted and depleted. She has built up her self-esteem, based not on what others think of her, but on what she thinks of herself. She is still working on her social skills, and her fear of rejection is the last hurdle to overcome - something that I am confident she will achieve.

Thousands of rising perfectionists, in many professions, are thankfully beginning to wonder if there is more to life than working 16 hours a day for the benefit of the bottom line – profit and the ability to buy a few more material possessions. So many people have an unbalanced life, where the demands for career success severely outweigh other, often more important aspects of their personal lives.

Setting a new lifestyle now

Have you ever smelt freshly picked lemongrass or freshly-mown grass, fresh-cut flowers or just-baked bread? These, as well as many others, are what I call natures perfumes.

- ***What do you think is the most beautiful sight in the world?***
  Open up your eyes and look. Is it what you are looking at right now?
- ***What do you think is the most important thing for you to do in your life?***
  Open up your mind. Is it what you are doing right now?
- ***Who do you think is the most important person in your life?***
  Open up your heart. Is it the person who is with you right now?

Many people never take the time to smell nature's perfumes or to identify what is beautiful or really important in their lives. Instead they focus on an alternative perfume - profit - or they put off the important things in life until tomorrow, which of course, as we know never comes.

The Taoist sages of ancient China draw our attention to nature because they see a creative power in it that humans seem to have lost touch with. Nature is the creative and beautiful expression of the impulse of the universe, which when humans align to it can share in its beauty and power.

Exercise 13 – spending time

Think about what you spend your time on now and how you would like to change this.

**% of my time spent now   %of my time I want to spend
How I can change this?**

Work

Family

Relationship

Friends

Personal growth

Hobbies/leisure

Spiritual self

Community

Knowing what really matters

Knowing what really matters and doing it at the right time is key to getting the right life balance and lifestyle. Think carefully about what really matters in your life and plan to prioritize this above all the other trivia that fills up your life.

- *What really matters at work?*
  Work that you love and that matches your values and beliefs
- *What really matters in your family?*
  Families mostly support and love us, but can also sometimes overwhelm us. Getting a bal-

ance between one's family and oneself is very important. Think enjoyment, not duty

- *What really matters in your relationships?*
  Don't' just say words of love – act them out also. Love is as love does!
- *What really matters with friends?*
  Having a terrific evening out with friends, writing letters of appreciation, or simply calling them and telling them you are thinking about them
- *What really matters in your personal growth?*
  Workshops, reading books and attending lectures can help us grow as individuals
- *What really matters regarding hobbies and leisure?*
  Taking a holi-hour (like holiday) for total relaxation between work can really help. It could mean reading a magazine, taking a walk or a quick shopping spree
- *What really matters to your spiritual self?*
  Positive energy that flows from a spiritual awareness so it might be worth exploring what your spiritual self is in terms of your passions, your values and your beliefs
- *What really matters in your contribution to society?*
  This area allows you to make your own special difference in the world. It is from this area that much of your self esteem and satisfaction in life can come. This could relate to your friends, family, community, your country, the world. Everyone is capable of contributing to the well being of this planet

Ten Tips for Developing Resilience for a Better Lifestyle

Resilience is the ability to keep a clear, unemotional head throughout stressful situations or upsetting experiences and recover quickly. Many clients come to me to find out how they can develop a resilience to their stressors. The first thing I say is 'actions speak louder than words'. When we are under acute stress, we simply don't think clearly and so all that theory we have learnt about managing stress disappears. We all manage our stresses differently. Some ways of managing them can be healthier than others. Without any real knowledge of how to best manage our stresses, we may fall into unhealthier patterns of coping such as avoiding, ignoring or running away; distorting reality or denying that we have stresses or worse using drugs or alcohol to temporarily 'forget' our stresses The problem is that these methods of coping with stress can lead to other health problems. Let us look now at healthier coping strategies for stress management.

1. Resilience through the way you think

'Your mind is like a fertile garden and for it to flourish, you must nurture it daily. Never let the weeds of negative thoughts (fear, guilt, sadness, pain) and actions take over the garden of your mind. Stand guard at the gateway of your mind. Keep it healthy and strong – it will work miracles in your life if you will only let it.' 'We have 60,000 thoughts each day and most of them are repetitive. So make those repetitive thoughts, happy positive thoughts not negative sad thoughts. "If you want joy/happiness then think joyful/happy thoughts. Catch yourself and stop thinking negative or painful thoughts. The Monk Who Sold His Ferrari – Robin Sharma

Better communications in relationships - relationships are a significant source of stress. Not being able to communicate properly, having difficulty handling conflict and failing to be assertive each give rise to stressful situations. For most people, learning how to be assertive, rather than aggressive, means being able to assess what they want and then finding a way of achieving them. Assertive responses require us to speak out and show our feelings, both negative and positive, rather than bottle up our thoughts and emotions. We also need to respect and value our own contribution to society. We will be looking further at how we can speak out effectively in chapter 9.

Re-appraising the situation - the most stressful aspect of a changing situation is not the change itself, but the anticipated impact of that change. Expectations, beliefs and assumptions are applied to a given situation and have a significant effect upon our capacity to embrace and adapt to change. Re-appraising means checking those assumptions and examining and restructuring our beliefs. It also means removing any distortions we have made and getting things into a more objective perspective – in other words, de-personalising the issue.

Talking to yourself - talking to yourself is not the "first sign of madness", but something which most of us do a lot of the time. For many people, self-talk is an effective defence against stress. Constructive self-talk allows us to avoid our negative interpretations of events and think positively about the situation. It also means focusing on alternative and positive views. *"What if I make a mess of it - I hate talking in groups - suppose people laugh at my ideas?" These* are the kind of negatives assumptions one could make about an unfamiliar situation. Constructive alternatives might be: *"This is a challenge - I can take a deep breath and relax as I stand up to speak - the Board will enjoy what I have to tell them - every time I do these presentations I get better at doing them"*

2. Resilience through improving your problem solving skills

Problem solving is one of the most difficult things to start but once tackled can reduce stress significantly. These are some tips for problem solving:

- Identifying the problem clearly, then collecting relevant facts which clarify the problem.
- Generating a range of alternative solutions through brainstorming ideas or looking at how

others have solved similar problems or asking experts to select an optimum alternative.
- Setting out an objective action plan which you can implement and re-evaluate as needed

3. Resilience through organizing your life

Organizing your life may seem an impossible nightmare. One client admitted to me that he hadn't sorted out his income tax in years, because he just could not face it. It wasn't because he didn't have the money, it was simply because he couldn't handle the organisational task of dealing with it. Filofaxes, mobile phones and laptops help organise us by incorporating diaries, phone and address books and data storage, but we still need to organise our minds first in order to organise the gadgets.

pattern planning – pattern planning is simply identifying what really matters to you and then ensuring, through rigorous logging, that you get these things done. A diary is essential for this. Plan to put into your diary all your regular appointments. You decide in advance what you perceive to be important enough to put into your diary, and then repeat these entries as appropriate. Examples include a regular work commitment, or the gym, or a hair appointment, or an important birthday or anniversary. In addition you could fit in less obvious things that may, nevertheless, be just as important to you: taking time for lunch with a friend, time to read or talk to the kids, time for your partner and, last but not least, time for yourself. While electronic diaries have bleeping or vibrating reminders, for the really important things I use a wonderfully non-technical gadget – the 'post it' note. A particularly popular computer company recognises this by having virtual post it notes for their screens!

4. Resilience through making the most of your time

"Yesterday is history, tomorrow a mystery, today a gift, that's why they call it the present" Anonymous.

The present is reading these very words now, but once read, those words change from the future to the past. By taking your life into your hands and being present, this can greatly enhance your life. "The greatest obstacle to living", according to philosopher, Seneca, "is waiting. Everything that will happen belongs to the domain of the uncertain: live now". Time seems to be something that one can never have enough of – it is constantly running through our fingers completely out of our control. But what we are in control of is how we spend our time. According to the famous philosopher Kant, time is the prerequisite of everything. What we call time is the succession of the past, the present and the future. But the past has gone and the future has not yet arrived. So everything that we experience happens in the present.

When we do not make the most of our time we:	When we do make the most of our time we:
Are chaotic, wasting time and resources	Are time and resource efficient
Are without priorities	Can set priorities
Only concentrate on one thing at a time	Can multi-task
Are easily distracted and impatient	Are focused
Are mostly reactive	Are proactive
Don't plan or judge time very well	Can plan and judge time well
Miss out on the important things	Can make time for the important things
Can't say 'No' and can't finish effectively	Can say 'No' and can finish effectively
Can't delegate	Can delegate as appropriate
Often procrastinate	Never procrastinate

Valuing time - by attaching a monetary value to your time, based on your salary or daily or hourly rate you can begin to understand how valuable time is. Then review each task and ask whether it is worth that value, or whether it is more appropriate to delegate it to someone else. Figure out what your three largest time wasters are and reduce them by 50%.

Creating more time for yourself, delegate and be sensitive to other people's time - taking the time to plan can free up more time for managing proactively rather than reactively.

Saying 'No' when you need to - remember the most important time saver is the ability to constructively say 'NO'.

If we ignore these tips then we can leave ourselves little time for pleasantries. This poem by W.H. Davies reminds me of this.

No Time   WH Davies

What is this life if, full of care, we have no time to stand and stare.

No time to stand beneath the boughs, and stare as long as sheep and cows.

No time to see, when woods we pass, where squirrels hide their nuts in grass.

No time to see, in broad daylight, streams full of stars like skies at night.

No time to turn at Beauty's glance, and watch her feet, how they can dance.

No time to wait 'til her mouth can enrich that smile her eyes began.

A poor life this if, full of care, we have no time to stand and stare

---

5. Resilience through setting goals for work/life

Making plans and setting goals are key behaviours for avoiding stress at work, particularly in career development, but they also have a place in your life with family and friends and in achieving personal fulfilment. By identifying goals, setting objectives, working out strategies and implementing action plans in each of these areas, the individual can avoid constantly having to react to situations as they occur. This gives a sense of control and empowerment.

6. Resilience through connecting to the right people

'Spend more time with those who make your life more meaningful. Revere special moments: revel in their power.' Robin Sharma

It is important to identify people you know who can assist you with your difficulties, provide emotional support, act as mentors and provide a listening ear.

7. Resilience through eating healthily

In Chapter 6, we looked at how important it is for the mind and body to be nurtured with the right chemicals. Most of these, as we have seen come from food but also increasingly drugs play a part in balancing mind and body. The right balance of proteins, carbohydrates and minerals in the form of a healthy, nutritious balanced diet is essential. The following tips for creating your uniquely healthy eating plan can help you with this.

10 tips for creating your unique healthy eating plan

This Healthy Eating Plan is about making healthy eating so enjoyable that you will not want to stop. The key to this programme for change is to eat nutritionally balanced foods only when you are hungry, to regularly exercise within a fitness programme and to start balancing your mental approach to life.

Nutritional Recommendations

These nutritional recommendations can help you design your own unique healthy eating and fitness plan, which fits into your lifestyle and helps you get to the weight you want.

1. **Make your eating/drinking and your life as enjoyable and as active as possible!**
2. **Increase the amount of pure water you drink.** You can rarely have enough of it but decrease the amount of water you drink through drinks with additives, caffeine and sugar, which unbalance blood glucose levels.
3. **Eat regularly and moderately, depending on your fitness routines and your metabolism** Also avoid snacking between meals unless you are feeling hungry.
4. **Increase your 'healthy' LGV carbohydrate consumption** E.g. wholegrain bread/rice/cereals, pasta, lentils, beans and other pulses, vegetables and fruit.

5. **Increase your fibre consumption**
   E.g. vegetables, pulses and fruit are good sources of fibre.

6. **Moderate/decrease your fat consumption**
   Eat unsaturated fat e.g. olive oil & soft margarine/cheeses, rather than saturated fats e.g. in meats, hard cheeses, butter, lard or cream.

7. **Ensure you have enough protein, but not too much.**
   Meat is not the only source of protein, some vegetables also contain it. Eat lean fish, chicken and offal, with red meats being a less frequent part of your diet.

8. **Decrease your 'less healthy' HGV carbohydrates**
   Sugary carbohydrates such as chocolate, sweets, alcohol/sugary drinks may unbalance your blood glucose levels. Fatty carbohydrates e.g. cakes, pastries, white bread and other refined foods, include extra, unnecessary fat.

9. **Have some pre-prepared 'healthy food and enjoyable meals'**
   Keep some in your freezer for when you feel too tired to bother to cook and have plenty of enticing healthy foods treats such as fruit (strawberries, grapes, low fat yoghurts) and drinks such as low fat/low sugar chocolate drinks or soft drinks and low alcohol drinks.

10. **Don't be too hard on yourself**
    You can't expect to change your eating habits instantly. Instead, gradually wean yourself off

your old habits whilst trying out the exciting food alternatives on offer.

8. Resilience through body fitness

People who exercise become stronger, fitter, sexier, have more energy and burn calories for longer. They are also at less risk of many illnesses such as osteoporosis (bone softening) or heart disease. There are many daily activities that constitute exercise - using the stairs instead of the lift; walking the last few stops of a bus journey; walking round the block instead of settling down to watch TV; washing the car instead of taking it to the car wash, gardening or growing your own organic food and having a more active sex life. This is what we call gaining functional fitness. So it is not all about deciding to run a marathon or spending your whole life in the gym. You could step up the pace of your exercise in a way that you feel comfortable with, by either introducing a workout into your daily activities or with brisk walking, jogging, cycling or swimming. Alternatively, subscribing to a gym is a great motivator, especially if you can invest in a personal trainer to get you started.

There are 3 key elements to an effective body fitness plan:-

- **Cardio-respiratory performance** – This improves the efficiency of the heart and lungs, which in turn means a better supply of food and oxygen carried in the blood to the muscles. This type of exercise is achieved through aerobic exercise such as running, cycling, swimming, tennis, squash and ball sports such as rugby or football, along with many other alternatives.

- **Strength/Endurance** - This increases the amount of force that a muscle can exert and the ability to repeat an action over and over again, or sustain muscular contraction. Strength/ endurance sports include rowing (either on water or on a machine), golf (play 18 holes at a rapid pace and carry your own bag), weight training, windsurfing and circuit training.
- **Flexibility** – This stretches the muscles and can be achieved through yoga, dance, The Alexander Technique, tai chi and swimming.

The following are different types of exercise which should be done ideally at least three times a week. The key is to find an exercise that you really enjoy rather than feeling it is your daily penance.

Power walking, jogging, cycling, dancing or swimming. Swimming is one of the best all-round forms of exercise because, not only is it aerobic and works many of the major muscle groups (you must vary the stroke), but the joints are protected from impact because the water bears the load. You are also exercising against the resistance of the water, so it is more efficient.

Working out in the gym is a great motivator. You can either work out on your own or with a personal trainer or with friends and other like minded people through the many group activities such as aerobic dance, yoga, spinning classes, circuit training etc.

The Green Gym involves exercise in the country-side or in open **spaces by taking part in conservation activities such as:** tree planting; creating school nature areas; hedge laying; fostering rare plants & animals or constructing dry stone walls, fences, gateways & styles. This type of exercise offers a way to get fit and healthy and provides an exciting alternative for people who do not like the idea of joining a sports centre or gym. As well as improving your health, by taking part you will have the opportunity to meet new people and learn new skills. There is also the satisfaction of making a difference to your community and environment.

Benefits of Exercise:

There are so many benefits to exercise. We were designed as human beings to move and that was the way cave men survived. Exercise is the key to keeping our body functioning to maximum capability.

These are some of the benefits of exercise:

- **Decreases appetite.** A degree of physical activity is necessary for appetite mechanisms to work properly. Those who do not exercise usually have larger appetites.
- **Boosts metabolic rate.** Vigorous exercise will raise metabolic rate for up to 15 hours.

- **Creates more muscle which speeds up metabolism.** Since muscle burns up more energy than fat, the more muscle you have, the quicker your metabolism is. Developing muscle through exercise, therefore, helps increase metabolism and improves stamina.
- **Has a positive effect on the mind,** giving you a general feeling of well being. Most GPs recognise the connection between being unfit and depression.
- **Creates more flexibility** and so less risk of muscle strain.
- **Creates more toned physique**
- **Creates more energy**
- **Improves quality of sleep**
- **Creates Stronger bones** so reduced risk of fractures.
- **Improves circulation**
- **Lowers blood pressure**, if it was high.
- **Creates a more efficient, fitter heart**

9. Resilience through mind fitness

So much money has been spent on body fitness and dieting over the years and yet it is only relatively recently that it has been realised how important mind fitness is. The old saying 'Use it or lose it' applies, as much to the mind as it does to the body. As children, we go to school and become accustomed to stretching our minds every day, but as adults we go to work and generally do the same things every day, which invariably does not challenge our minds. Watching TV at night may not always be mind challenging – it depends on what we watch. We then wonder why our memory is not so good, or why we don't seem to be able to solve problems or calculate things as quickly as we did when we were younger. Its seems also that we leave ourselves less time to sleep. Either we go to bed later with so much to do or get up earlier to go to our demanding jobs. On top of that our sleep is often less beneficial as we go to bed stressed or with so many things on our minds. Let us have a look at how we can achieve mind fitness in the face of all these difficulties.

Better sleep for mind fitness

I have so many clients who come to me complaining of their lives being upset by not being able to sleep. Usually this is linked with going through a difficult period, where there are too many decisions and worries that are hounding them for them to manage a restful night.

Peter was going through a really bad stage in his life. He came to me looking shattered and dejected. His wife was an alcoholic and she left him to look after their three teenage children as well as doing his full time job. He felt he was living in a nightmare of trying to keep his employers happy, run his kids around and keep his often drunk wife at bay. Quite naturally, he found himself awake at night trying to work out how he could keep juggling all the responsibilities in his life. He would then worry that he could not get back to sleep and had to be up at five every morning to sort the kids out for school before getting to work at 8am. Often he was awake at 3am and would not get back to sleep again. He got up at 5am *with a huge knot in his stomach and would jump onto his exercise bike for twenty minutes to try to unknot it. He said he could not go to bed earlier as he had too much to do in the evenings, although he did admit to falling asleep in the chair quite often.*

We need 9.5 hours sleep a night or we may become clumsy, stupid, unhappy, or even dead.

Lack of sleep is itself a source of stress. It produces a wide range of cognitive, behavioural and physiological deficits, which, in turn, reduce one's capacity to respond effectively to pressure.

Dr Coren, in his book Sleep Thieves, said that 'Evolution has really programmed us to require a lot more sleep than we typically get'. He saw Edison's light bulb as being to blame for this, with data from 1910, prior to its invention, showing that people were sleeping around nine to nine and a half hours per night. Edison, who considered sleeping a waste of time, invented the light bulb to allow him to work at night when he could not sleep. He did, however, nap a lot and the reality was that with his naps he was mostly getting eight hours sleep out of each 24. It was also known that Churchill and Margaret Thatcher were great nappers.

If we lose two hours sleep per day, after 5 days we could be borderline retarded.
Dr Coren explains that sleep is governed by a 12 hour circadian cycle, with the greatest compulsion to sleep between 1 - 4 am and 1 - 4 pm. 'It is probably the case that evolution wanted us to sleep in two bites', he said. 'A big bite of eight to eight and a half hours at night and a smaller bite of two to two and a half hours during the afternoon.' But he says,

'If you're losing two hours [sleep] each day, then at the end of five days, you'll be ten hours sleep-deprived, and you're going to act as if you're 15 points dumber in terms of IQ'. He explains how junior doctors in the US worked 96 hours per week - often turning themselves into diagnosis-giving, prescription-writing, surgery-performing zombies.

Peter came to me with his sleep problems after taking on a particularly difficult project at work. I suggested that we look at how he could improve his sleep patterns. We looked at his lifestyle, both at work and at home, and I suggested ways that he could separate his work life from his home life more definitively. He had been used to his boss calling him up in the evening to discuss work, and his kids or wife calling him up during the day while he was at work. I suggested he tell his family that they only call him in emergency. Then get his secretary to take messages if they did call. With regards to his boss calling in the evening, I suggested he put his phone on to answer phone. We looked at how he could rearrange his home tasks and even include the kids in some of them, so that he had more time to relax in the evenings in preparation for sleeping, and time to go to bed earlier if possible, which would gain him some sleep time. We addressed his waking up during the night, and I suggested him doing some meditation and breathing exercises, or having some novels at hand to read. This would stop his mind wandering towards his daily agenda and he would be more likely to feel tired and go back to sleep. After a few months he said he felt completely re-energised.

If you suffer from sleep problems, try:-

- Only going to bed when you are tired.
- Take more exercise during the day.
- Avoid heavy eating, stimulants or working just before bed.
- Have a warm bath just before bed and make sure the bed is warm and comfortable.
- Keep the bedroom clutter-free and calm, while minimising noise and light.

Mind games for mind fitness

Why not incorporate some mind challenging activities into your day? This could involve doing the (now trendy} Sudoku puzzles or computer brain training or the traditional crossword puzzles in your newspaper, playing poker or chess, taking a challenging evening class, reading more or deciding to write your memoirs. All of these things will stimulate those brain neurons and get them buzzing.

Visualisation for mind fitness

Mental relaxation can be achieved through visualisation. It requires us to imagine, in detail, a familiar scene, which is associated with peace and happiness. This, for me, is a hot sunny day - I can feel the sun beating down on me, hear the sea rolling beside me, and touch the soft warm sand around me. For others it might be standing on top of a mountain.

'Take time to meditate on something you love (the sea or a rose), smell the fragrance and see the beauty, look into it and envision your preferred life.' 'If it is joy you prefer, then envision yourself laughing or having fun with your friends. Laughter opens your heart and soothes your soul. When you run inspiring, imaginative pictures through the movie screen of your mind, wonderful things start to happen in your life. Then take the time to improve your thoughts and your life towards that goal. Associate pleasure with good habits and pain with bad ones. Also create positive peer pressure to keep you inspired ie tell people. Then set a time line. Three aspects to realizing your image: how you see yourself, how others see you and the truth. Know the truth.' The Monk Who Sold His Ferrari – Robin Sharma

Meditation for mind fitness

Meditation facilitates the development of a peaceful view of life, by encouraging us to focus on a single object or experience - "a mantra" or single word or phrase, which is repeated over and over again. A simple mantra is Ham-sa. In Sanskrit it means I am that, I am divine, I am with God. It is pronounced Hahhhm as you breathe in and Sahhhhh as you breath out. The idea of behind these techniques is to free our minds of all current stresses and allow mind and body to really relax for a time. We can do any of these techniques ourselves at any time of the day, in order to both relax and energise ourselves. It is important, however, is that a peaceful place can be found with no likely interruptions. If there is nowhere else, there is always a bathroom!

Relaxation for mind fitness

Deep muscle relaxation induces a state of deep physical relaxation by relaxing each of your major muscle groups in turn. You can decide whether to sit down with your feet on the floor and arms supported, or, if you have the space, you can lie down on the floor. Go back to chapter one for this exercise is the same as the vision of purpose one.

Massage has been practised in the Middle and Far East since at least 3000 BC. Hippocrates wrote in the 5th century BC: '*The way to health is to have a scented bath and an oiled massage each day.*' Massage includes Swedish massage, aromatherapy, acupressure, shiatsu and reflexology. Oil is still used for all forms of massage. Aromatherapy uses essential concentrated oils extracted from plants. Reflexologists believe that gentle massage and manipulation of the feet, which are linked through meridians to various organs in the body, can 'unblock', so giving both physical and emotional benefits. They say just walking bare foot on grass, sand, or earth can be almost as good as a session with them. Massage:

- **Relaxes** our body and mind and so relieves the strains and stresses of our daily life.
- **Improves circulation** and our muscular and nervous systems, and also helps our body to assimilate food and get rid of waste.
- **Calms and soothes** and helps people with depression or anxiety, allowing them to deal more constructively with everyday worries and problems, and to regain self-confidence..

Breathing exercises for mind fitness

How often do we breathe properly, especially in the face of stress? Breathing is so important for relaxation and so easy to do. Simply find somewhere quiet and lie or sit in a relaxed position. Then close your eyes and take in a deep breath. Count to eight slowly in your head whilst breathing in, then breathe out equally slowly, counting to eight again. Do this for as long as is necessary and you will find the results rewarding.

10. Resilience to extreme crisis stress

I have seen hundreds of victims of extreme crises/ disasters and singularly the most important thing that helps relieve their sudden acute feelings of being stressed and overwhelmed is to find out that the reactions they are suffering over those first few weeks are normal and usually only temporary. I then help them process, understand and get some meaning out of what has happened to them. Finding meaning and positivity from it are essential to recovery and, as we have already discussed throughout this book, there have been many positive things that my clients have gained from their experiences.

These are a few tips I give on managing crisis stress:

- Keep life as normal as possible through your crisis.
- Acknowledge that you have had an abnormal and extreme experience.
- Understand your normal stress reactions to crisis.
- Talk about your crisis to a good, caring listener, in order to gain support and find ways to process or resolve it. Friends or family are often the first people to call on, but if this is difficult try the many telephone/internet help lines or arrange to see a counsellor.
- Focus on your issues and think of solutions.
- Visit your doctor if you feel stressed, depressed or unable to cope.

The Kaizen (Japanese word for improvement) philosophy on life, I believe, summarizes this chapter best. Whilst Kaizen is mostly associated with productivity improvement in manufacturing, it is also used as daily rituals for the purpose of individual improvement.

10 Kaizen tips for radiant living

1. **Peace/Solitude:** Meditation -15 minutes of silence and solitude
2. **Physicality:** Yoga or exercise
3. **'Live' nourishment:** Live foods. Foods that have enjoyed nature, sun, rain, soil. eg vegetables
4. **Abundant knowledge:** Lifelong learning. Knowledge is potential power. Keep reading. Books help you find what is already within yourself (the self you were as a young child).
5. **Personal reflection:** Written reflection of the day. Are they positive? If yes then develop them. If negative then stop doing them. Ask yourself what you would do today if this was your last day then envision this and if possible do it!
6. **Early Awakening:** It is quality of sleep not quantity. First and last ten minutes of the day are the most important to think positive thoughts. They must be calm. Get up with the sun. Being in the sun rejuvenates and keeps you mind bright and restores you to physical and emotional vibrancy. The sun is thought to be a connection to the soul.
7. **Music and laughter:** Music: makes you laugh. It makes you dance. It makes you sing. It lifts your spirit. Laughter: the average child laughs 300 times a day whilst the average adult only 15 times. Laughing is the medicine of the soul. Laugh even if you don't feel like it – it will make you feel happier. Laugh, play, and give thanks for all you have.

8. **The Spoken Word:** Self talk for strength, focus and happiness through mantras eg.
   For motivation repeat 'I am inspired, disciplined and energized' 2 or 3 hundred times.
   For self-confidence repeat 'I am strong, able and calm' a few hundred times.
   Sow a thought and reap an action. Reap an action and you sow a habit. Sow a habit and you reap a character. Sow a character and you reap a destiny (Yogi Raman). By filling your mind with words of hope you become more hopeful. By filling up your mind with words of kindness you become kind and so on with courage.

9. **Congruent Character:** Living in a manner congruent to these virtuous principles. Honesty, patience, industry, compassion, humility and courage leads to a congruence of character.

10. **Simplicity:** To reduce ones needs and make life less complicated.'

Remember this quote below and the above rituals both come from *The Monk Who Sold His Ferrari – Robin Sharma*

'To install a new habit takes at least 21 days (time to develop a new neural pathway). Throw as much energy as you can to developing this new habit. And enjoy the process. Fear is a conditioned response: a life-sucking habit that can easily consume your energy, creativity and spirit if you are not careful. Beat off fear whenever it appears and do what you fear.'

Pickle Jar theory of Life Style Balance

The following theory for a lifestyle balance has been around for a while but I believe it is even more relevant to today. So with some editing I present it to you. I use pebbles in the jar as, situated by the sea, they protect our precious land and homes from the ever-rolling waves.

A professor stood before his philosophy class. He picked up a large empty jar and proceeded to fill it with pebbles. He then asked the students if the jar was full? They agreed that it was. He then poured some glass marbles into the jar. The marbles rolled into the open areas between the pebbles. He then asked the students again if the jar was full. They agreed it was. Next, he poured some sand into the jar. Of course, the sand filled up everything else. He then asked once more if the jar was full. The students responded with a unanimous: "YES!" Finally he produced 2 glasses of wine from under the table and proceeded to pour the entire contents into the jar, effectively filling the empty space between the sand. The students laughed that it was now definitely full.

"Now," said the professor, as the laughter subsided, "I want you to recognise that this jar represents your life. The pebbles are the important things – your family, your health, your children, your friends – things that if everything else was lost and only they remained, your life would still be full. The glass marbles are the other things that matter like your job or your home. The sand is everything else – the small stuff" (hobbies, politics, material wealth, cleaning etc.) He continued: "If you put the marbles or the sand into the jar first, there is no room for the pebbles. Take time for the things that are critical to your happiness and wellbeing. Play with your children. Take time to get medical checkups. Take your partner out dancing. You can then make time to go to work, clean the house, and play golf. Take care of the pebbles first – the things that really matter. The rest is just sand." But then one of the students raised her hand and enquired what the wine represented. The professor smiled and said: "I'm glad you asked. It just goes to show you that no matter how full your life may seem, there's always room for a couple of glasses of wine!"

8. Leap of Faith

Those who follow a faith normally choose one suited to their own moral code and cultural background. Some may choose a faith outside of themselves such as a faith in a religion or a political party, a sovereign or a spiritual leader. For others, they choose to have faith in themselves. Whatever faith they choose, it gives them the courage, strength and resilience to act for their goals in the face of any of life's challenges and tragedies.

When I went to help the Thai people of Kao Lak in Phuket, a few years ago following the horrific Tsunami that had killed hundreds of thousands of their people, I was impressed at how much faith they had. Most followed the Buddhist religion and had faith that their lost loved ones were going on to a better life. Their homes and possessions had been utterly destroyed, but because materialism wasn't their God, they had the faith to start again from nothing to rebuild their lives. While doing so, they still had concern, gratitude and compassion for those of us who were trying our best to help them.

Kimi was a retailer of food and household goods in a small shop which was situated on one of the roads off the Kao Lak shore. She would normally have been selling her goods to the many tourists who would pass on their way to and from the beautiful Kao Lak beach. But on that fateful day of the Tsunami she not only lost her livelihood when her shop was swamped, but had also lost her father and her brothers, who had been by the shoreline mending their fishing boats when the Tsunami struck. When she saw the huge wave she had run for her life, away from her shop and managed to get out of harms way. As a Buddhist who believed in reincarnation, she consoled herself with the thought that her lost relations would live a better life next time.

When I was there, six months after the Tsunami, I would see her sitting each day outside of her mostly empty, damaged shop. She had only a fraction of her original stock and there were none of her regular tourists or visitors passing by. Yet, she optimistically told me that things would get better again one day.

She kept reminding me how much she appreciated the young volunteers from all over the world, who were helping her and her fellow citizens, to rebuild their homes and their livelihoods from scratch.

Not all people, however, see faith so positively – indeed, religion has been the cause of much divisiveness and hatred amongst nations and peoples, causing many bloody slaughters for the sake of religious supremacy. Let us have a brief look at some insights into the power and betrayal of religion towards the people they served.

The power and betrayal of religion as a faith

Religious faith has been around for many thousands of years, beginning with the multiple God pagan faith of the ancient Egyptians and their ancestors. Each God had a different role as part of a myth or story that was created to explain life's mysteries and disasters in order to make them bearable – from how the earth was created, why the seasons change, through complex relationship issues, to the enigma of death. These ancient people believed that their nation's leaders were the important human link between these Gods and themselves. Alexander the Great, who was Greek (356-323BC) conquered Persia and Egypt and influenced each of their faiths with Greek culture and myths. The two main cultures that existed around that time were the Indo-European and Semitic culture.

The Indo-European culture, which the Greeks and the Romans belonged to, was part of an Eastern mysticism (which was to influence Hinduism, Buddhism and Chinese religions).

The Semitic culture, which originated from the Arabian Peninsula, was part of a Western mysticism (which was to influence Judaism, Christianity and Islamic religions).

Around 4BC, Jesus was born and developed great powers of healing. He explained his teachings through myths or parables and preached that one should love one's neighbour and enemies, having compassion for the weak and the poor, and forgiving those who have sinned. The Jewish religious leaders of the time, however, felt threatened by Jesus' humble yet powerful teachings and the Romans, who were ruling at the time, condemned him to death by crucifixion. A few days after his death, rumours spread that he had been resurrected and was therefore no ordinary man and must be the 'Son of God'. Be it myth or history, Jesus' name and teachings grew in popularity from there on.

Christianity was later taken up by the Roman Empire as its official religion. Many scholars claim that the Romans literally stole Jesus from his original followers, hence using him to expand their own power. Constantine commissioned and financed a new

Bible, which embellished those gospels that made Jesus Godlike. The Christian church then devalued the power of the ancient Mother Goddess and, therefore, the social importance of women. Christian education moved away from the public places into closed convents, cathedrals and monasteries. In doing so, Christianity ensured that education was offered only to a chosen few – namely privileged males. This allowed Christian leaders to establish a social dominance over the masses throughout medieval times.[2]

---

2 **The Dead Sea Scrolls** and Coptic Scrolls, which were discovered in the late 1940s and early 1950s, spoke, however, of Christ's ministry in very human terms. The Vatican tried to suppress the release of these scrolls, as they confirmed that the modern Bible had been compiled and edited by men whose political agenda was to convert the sun-worshipping pagans to Christianity. By incorporating pagan symbols, dates and rituals into the growing Christian faith, the Roman Emperor, Constantine, created a kind of hybrid religion that was acceptable to both parties. Egyptian sun discs became the halos of the Catholic saints. Pictograms of the goddess Isis nursing her miraculously conceived son Horus became the blueprint for our modern images of the Virgin Mary nursing Baby Jesus. And virtually all elements of the Catholic ritual – the mitre, the altar, and the communion - were taken directly from pagan religions. The god Mithras, worshipped by a cult Roman religion, was born on December 25th, died and was buried in a rock tomb, and then resurrected in three days. December 25th is also the birthday of the Egyptian god Osiris and the Greek gods Adonis and Dionysus. Originally Christianity honoured the Jewish Sabbath of Saturday, but Constantine shifted it to coincide with the pagan's veneration day of the sun – SUNday!

Power of Man

Renaissance humanists and philosophers from the 15th to 16th centuries then focussed more on the power of man, as a reaction to centuries of Christian totalitarianism Individualism started to be voiced and more personal freedom began to be demanded. The bible was translated from Latin into English, so that it wasn't exclusive to priests and educated people and with the aid of the printing press (invented in the 1450s), the movement was able to grow like never before. At around the same time, science was breaking away from religion.

Scientific theories were developed around the 17th century, which challenged creationism in favour of evolution. Isaac Newton (1642-1726) developed the Law of Gravity and Laws of Motion. From these laws, machines were invented which led to the Industrial Revolution in the 18th and 19th centuries and the development of the computer technology of the 20th and 21st centuries. Darwin proved that humans had evolved from primates, rather than having been created in their present state by God. Science today still forces us to question religion. The huge popularity of Richard Dawkins' book *The God Delusion* shows how millions of people are individually questioning religion.

Spiritual faith however, today still seems to offer a meaningful and purposeful social and moral framework for many to live by. Studies have shown that spiritually conscious people report feeling happy and more satisfied with life than their non-spiritual counterparts. Faith creates a feeling of belonging and acceptance and can also offer hope in the face of adversity, suffering and death, helping people to cope with personal crises and traumatic events. Studies have shown that families with strong religious beliefs often have a lower rate of delinquency, alcohol and drug abuse and failed marriages – religious families even have lower incidences of illness and early death. In the face of such adversity, some, however, can temporarily lose their faith.

Mary came to me after the tragic death of her husband following an unexpected heart attack. She had been a deeply religious woman throughout her life, and her religion had been of great comfort to her throughout many challenges she had faced. But her husband's death had been too much for her and she had felt very angry with God for not having given them any warning signs about his heart condition. The negative stories that were emerging about her Roman Catholic faith had been a gradual concern for her for a while, but she had never thought of giving it up until now. She came to me very depressed, saying that she felt that her life had become empty and shallow.

We talked about what her religion had offered her and her husband in the past. We also talked about what her husband would have wanted her to do. She realised that he would have wanted her to continue her work with the church and to take comfort and companionship from others in the congregation. Her anger gradually subsided as she came to terms with the tragedy of losing her husband, and she eventually returned to her faith.

A world without religion

A vast number of people, who are questioning existing Western religions, are opting instead for having faith in themselves. Statistics show that only 1 billion out of 5 billion people across the world are currently sincere believers in religion.

Anais Nin commented over 30 years ago that faith was what we seem to lack most, and yet it was also what we seemed to be hungriest for:

> 'As we evolved into a new consciousness and clarity and clairvoyance, seeing through certain dogmas and certain hypocrisies and certain traditions that we didn't want, there came with this lucidity also a fear and great loneliness and a loss of faith'

She believed that we must, instead, have the faith to turn to ourselves as a creative piece of work. She noted that the artist would say: *'Although the world is like this, if I don't like it, I can change it.'*. And it is because the artist believes that life is changeable, that it can be metamorphosed and that it can be conquered.

Faith in self-awareness and therapies

In an increasingly stressful, unsupportive and disconnected world, individual and collective neurosis has increased, leading to the growing popularity, acceptability and take-up of psychological therapies. The British Association of Counselling and Psychotherapy has grown to a membership of over 32,000 with particular growth in sectors such as the work place (via Employee Assistance provision), the local community (via NHS GP surgery) and hospital provision.

There seems now to be a preoccupation with self-development and the healing of body and mind. Shopping malls, health clubs and the therapist's consulting room are taking over from churches as places for our daily worship. Yoga, martial arts and meditation have replaced prayer. And yet, many people still feel an inner emptiness, within their hollow communities.

Despite the media choosing to concentrate mostly on criticisms of many psychological therapies, an increasing number of people have been prepared to have faith in them. Geri Halliwell, Robbie Williams, Kate Moss and many more celebrities have admitted to and promoted the value of healing body and mind through methods such as yoga, meditation and counselling, and in doing so have given these therapies a 'pop' credibility.

Therapists, who stand by their professional code of ethics, do not seek power over their clients, as did most religious priests. Instead, they aim to serve them in a non-judgmental, empathic, caring and client-centred way. They are available to the community, as was the church once was, and often work on a voluntary basis or for fees that suit the client's pocket. Therapy, like the ideals of religion, helps people to love and respect themselves and, in doing so, move beyond themselves in order to love, respect and help others, both in their families and the wider community.

The relationship between client and therapist is, however, only a therapeutic one – not a real relationship. Whilst I have already spoken about an increasing number of virtual or pseudo relationships emerging, I believe that we must try to move back towards real relationships, real families and real communities.

This obsession with self-awareness and therapies, may have been in order to attain an inner peace. Pirsig, author of *Zen and the Art of Motorcycle Maintenance*, writes that inner peace involves:

- Physical quietness (stillness)
- Mental quietness (no wandering thoughts)
- Value quietness (no wandering desires but simply performing the acts of life).

Pirsig goes on to say that Zen Buddhists just sit as their form of meditation. When you are at one with your surroundings, then you have inner peace of mind, which produces good values, good thoughts, good actions and spiritual reality. Pirsig believed that we must start with our own heart, head and hands.

'We should be satisfied with our work, our craft and be at one with nature. On holiday, we are at one with the sun, the sea, love and family. But why are we now having to pay for what used to be the very basis of living? Because the technical revolution has taken us away from these things and replaced them with a material greed. Such is the pressure of work that we do not even have time to enjoy the basics, creating empty homes and empty hearts'. Pirsig

Alan Watts, in his book, The Book On the Taboo Against Knowing Who You Are, asks: 'What is the cause of the illusion that the self is a separate ego housed in a bag of skin that confronts a universe of physical objects that are alien to it. Rather a person's identity or ego binds them to the physical universe, creating a relationship with their environment and other people.

He explains that the separation of the self and the physical world leads to the misuse of man's natural environment leading to its destruction.

Eckhart Tolle says 'Non-resistance is the key to the greatest power in the universe. Through it, consciousness (spirit) is freed from its imprisonment in form. Inner non-resistance to form whatever it is or happens – is denial of the absolute reality of form.

Resistance endows the world and the ego with a heaviness and an absolute importance that makes you take yourself and the world very seriously. The play of form is then misperceived as a struggle for survival, and when that is your perception it becomes your reality.'

Tolle says that many things that happen to us are of a transient nature - events, situations, thoughts, emotions, desires, ambitions, fears, drama... they come, pretend to be all-important, and before you know it they are gone, dissolved into the no-thingness out of which they came. Were they ever real? Were they ever more than a dream?

When death approaches we may look back on our life and wonder if it was just another dream.

To awaken within the dream is our purpose now. When we are awake within the dream, the ego-created earth drama comes to an end and a more benign and wondrous dream occurs.

This, Tolle believed was 'The joy of being'. He went on to explain that true happiness cannot come to you through any possession, achievement, person or event – through anything that happens. It emanates from who you are.

- Peace comes about through inner non resistance to events - Zen 'Is that so?'
- Peace comes about through the wisdom of non judgement – Zen 'Maybe'
- Peace comes through the wisdom of impermanence – 'This, too, will pass' which leads to nonattachment. Once you see and accept the transience of all things you can enjoy the pleasures of the world whilst they last without fear of loss or anxiety about the future.

Tolle believes that non-resistance, non-judgment and non-attachment are the three aspects of true freedom and enlightened living. 'When you are no longer totally identified with forms, consciousness – who you are – becomes freed from its imprisonment in form. This freedom is the arising of inner space. It comes as a stillness, a subtle peace deep within you, even in the face of something seemingly bad.'

Tolle also comments on object and space consciousness: 'Object consciousness needs to be balanced by space consciousness. Space consciousness represents not only freedom from ego, but also from dependency on the things of this world, from materialism and materiality.' It is the spiritual dimension which alone can give transcendent and true meaning to this world.

Faith in oneself – self-belief

For some people it is a strong faith in themselves that sustains them. Self-belief and individuality has increasingly taken over from religious faith in the last few centuries. There was a real growth in humanism in the first half of the 20th century, led by Carl Rogers, Abraham Maslow, Aldous Huxley and others. In the 1960s and 70s self-theory and counselling became increasingly popular. People were encouraged to become autonomous individuals, with the emphasis on spontaneity, direct intimacy and awareness of reality.

David had strong self-belief and a drive to make money. His determination led him, at the age of 18, to create his own successful business as a service provider for the commercial world. Unlike his parents, he had no faith in religion. He chose instead to apply his own rules to life, and usually ruled others according to his own vision, too. He worked seven days a week developing his business. For relaxation he followed exercise rituals in his luxury gym, spent his money in the supermarkets and shopping malls and created his own community through social activities, usually by paying for other people's drinks. Despite having a loving family, he had numerous affairs and eventually was found out by his wife, who then ordered him out of the house. His desire to make money so outweighed everything else that he ended up letting go of his family and was left alone, with only his money and his rather needy 'friends' for company. Eventually, he came to me feeling lost and lonely, saying he had been close to ending his life.

We looked at what his core values and purpose had been when he was younger. He said that he had felt that he had always wanted to do things for people in hospital, but he had been too busy and had left the charity work to his wife, who had more time. He then told me that he loved music and had always dreamed of either playing in a band or becoming a DJ. He still had a passion for his business, but decided to spend less time there. Instead, he took time out to visit the sick in his local hospital and eventually became a DJ there. He also told me at a later session that he had donated money to an Alzheimer's charity, realising how devastated he had been when his mother had died from the disease. For fun, he had even started up his own band.

Faith in pride and passion are strong human drives and for those this can alone be sufficient faith. Pride and passion has moved artists like Michelangelo, architects like Christopher Wren, designers like Jonathan Ive and other talented craftsmen to create the most exquisite art, buildings, computers and other amazing artefacts. At one time, society was full of passion and pride in work - passion and pride to make the best quality furniture; passion and pride to create buildings and interiors with intricate detail and beauty; passion and pride to produce clothes that were lovingly hand sewn. There were no accountants or quality control masters, counting costs, time and productivity. They just weren't issues of the day. What was far more important, then, Robert M. Pirsig *said*, was real quality, as opposed to today's shallow quality. He said:

'We have shallow art and shallow technology, shallow living. We have lost our gravity. We need a reunification of real art and technology (techne means art) and spirituality. Quality is divine, it is good, it is God. God is passion, it is belief, it is positive attachment. Quality control is a means to an end and is self serving to those who manufacture. Manufacturing process is dehumanizing (tiny cog in large wheel). Instead of manically obsessing with what looks good to get peace of mind one should culture ones inner peace of mind so that inner good can emerge. It can occur in meditation or concentration of thought. It involves a lack of self-consciousness, which produces a complete identification with ones circumstances. A master craftsman has patience, care and attentiveness but more than that he has inner peace of mind which results from a kind of harmony with the work in which there is no leader and no follower. The material and the craftsman's thoughts change together in a progression of smooth, even changes until his mind is at rest at the exact instant which the material is right. Ie the subject and object are one'. Pirsig

Faith in the Internet

What seems to be most worshipped now is the powerful and mystical Internet. The Internet or 'Global Village' or 'Worldwide Web', as it is often called, exists within most of the world's computers and yet it is also outside of them - just as Spinoza, the Renaissance philosopher, described God.

We looked, in chapter 6, at how neurons are essential for the functioning of the amazingly complex human body and how they do it via an on-off basis of electrical impulses. Similarly our now amazingly complex computers operate on an on-off (0-1) basis of the binary system. And it is through the internet that both have become intimately connected.

The Internet already influences our every living moment. It is difficult to comprehend the power of the Internet, just as those in the past could not comprehend the power of God. Could the Internet be a vehicle for 'God' or 'good', as Jesus was 2000 years ago and the Gods were before him? I'm sure the internet would have blown Descarte's mind, who said that God had made living beings based on mechanical laws.

There are already hundreds of millions of people across the world using the Internet and its users are growing at a rapid rate. The internet enables us to communicate interactively with people all over the world in milliseconds. It gives us instant access to more knowledge than we ever dreamed possible. We can store all our data up in the clouds in what they call sky drive. Where does it go, I always wonder, and how much data can the sky eventually take? But we keep uploading. Despite this, so far the internet's reputation has been far from 'good'. It has had some very bad publicity, showing up the worst parts of human nature, most notably that of abusing and exploiting children. Perhaps we can change this shadowy reputation and begin to use the internet beyond images and twitters, for good instead of for bad. To use it as a forum for peace, warmth and compassion.

We can reach out to developing countries more than we do now, through the internet, to further help educate those people in remote areas on issues such as health, deadly diseases, growing nutritious food and many other aspects of basic survival. We can use it as a means to redistribute our terrible inequality of wealth, voluntarily transferring a small portion of our income to those across the world in desperate need. We can use it to encourage others to volunteer and support charities, both nationwide and across the world. Its potential is vast and I leave you to think about how else it might be used for the sake of Go(o)d, compassion and peace.

Faith to Leap
Perhaps for those of us who do not, therefore, believe in a Godhead or other religious faiths, we need at least to have faith to leap to what we believe in even if it is solely in our individual integrity, self reliance, passion, self respect and respect for others.

According to Anais Nin, we must act according to our values and purpose. Existentialists, including Nietzsche and Sartre, believed that people must have faith in themselves as a creative piece of work. We can decide:

- Who we are and what our unique values and beliefs are in relation to the rest of the world
- The ethics by which we want to live
- Whether we want to apply our human qualities of warmth, affection, generosity and compassion for people's physical health, happiness and peace of mind or
- Whether we want to choose a path of selfishness, greed, competitiveness, anger, hatred and destruction in order to gain what we want

But by having individual self-belief, can we be sure that we are as calm and happy as those who have faith in religions? Can we develop the same inner discipline that helps combat our negative states of mind and that can bring peace and unity into this world?

Philosophers such as Socrates, Plato and Aristotle, over 2000 years ago, highlighted the value of human warmth, affection, generosity and compassion together with the need for a life balance in order to gain physical health, happiness and peace of mind. Many philosophers, psychologists and religious leaders since have reiterated these teachings. The

Dalai Lama, today, still believes that warmth, affection and compassion are the essences of all religious teachings.

Who Has Taken the Leap of Faith?

The Psychiatrist in *The Dice Man*, took the leap of faith towards a life guided by the dice, abandoning a life of mediocrity. Taking this leap of faith (as quoted in Chapter 1) led to his eventual demise.

Jan took a leap of faith when she decided to break up with her husband of 20 years, Ed. She created a home and a new life for herself, just the way she wanted it – through love and compassion: through forming loving connections and through loving herself.

Anthony took a leap of faith, when he realised how important spending time playing with his children was, after he had nearly died in the pleasure boat tragedy.

Catherine Bailey and Katherine Ward both took a leap of faith when they decided to do what each of us has the freedom to do - to end our lives at any point.

Caroline took a leap of faith, after years of despair and attempted suicides, when she decided to stay alive and to struggle with her depression towards a happier and more connected life.

Gillian Hicks took a leap of faith when she decided to overcome her disabilities following the London bombing, and learnt how to walk and how to live again.

Emily Craddock took a leap of faith when she joined Greenpeace activist ship, knowing that each mission would have its dangers. For her, sadly, it meant dying at an early age.

My own Leap of Faith

I end this chapter with my own leap of faith. I was brought up having religious faith, but then turned away from it, towards self-belief, having chosen to be educated in science. But facing life's challenges my self-belief then dwindled and I turned to therapy to help me. Becoming a Counselling Psychologist, I then worked with many major tragic incidents, as well as many individual sudden deaths. I have, therefore, had plenty of time to contemplate both the negative and the positive effects that arise from brushing with death. I even had my own experience.

On a boating holiday I got back to the marina very late alone after staying on at a party. I mounted the gangplank to the boat I was staying on, rather unsteadily and slipped into the seawater. I found that I couldn't get back up onto the boat and screamed out to my friends to help me but they didn't wake. I struggled for a while but then felt extremely tired.

Somehow the water, on that summer evening in Majorca, seemed warm and enticing. I began to sink lower and lower just feeling supremely comfortable and sleepy. Then, with a sudden and huge spurt of energy I pushed myself back up out of the water and screamed like I had never done in my life. This awoke my friends and they rushed out to pull me out. On that day, I had opted for life, and in doing so, addressed the value of my own life, which at that time had been in a state of flux, having just separated from my long-term husband!

From then on I have always been interested in the mysteries of life and death. There are, however, so many mysteries yet to unfold in this world that our simple, undeveloped brains cannot yet comprehend. We are therefore left with faith in what we want to believe.

I believe in synchronicity – that is the gift of coincidence. I don't really believe there is a God but instead there is Go(o)d and there are Angels of Go(o)d. I believe that souls enter new lives and that Angels or free souls are awaiting their next rebirth. Also that, whilst they wait, they can help us humans on earth. They guide synchronicity towards us.

I believe that we are responsible for creating our own rich pattern of life, which is weaved from our life's experiences. Some have a simple pattern and others have a more intricate or less happy or more successful pattern. It is up to us how detailed and complex our pattern is or how much suffering or happiness it entails. How connected or lonely we are. Life does not have to be happy, however, to be beautiful. Man can get personal satisfaction out of selecting the various strands that created their unique pattern. Things of course still do happen to create suffering, pain, loneliness, sadness, hurt, hate but it is up to us to move that suffering back to happiness, connectivity, comfort and love. To reset our pattern to one we want to end up with.

9. Dare to Speak

By now, I hope you may feel like shouting about how you want to live, love, laugh and be happy. But if you find it difficult or even impossible to communicate well then your cause is lost.

Do you have the courage to speak out? Do you have the wisdom to know when only to listen?

Communication is not who you are, but how you act. Many people are too shy or lack the confidence to 'speak out' in front of a crowd, fearing rejection or humiliation. 'Yes' people (and that is most of us) are so busy saying 'Yes' to other people's requests that they have no time to speak out for themselves.

Jack *came to me saying that it had been suggested by his company that he come to counselling, to find out why he had become so aggressive at work. He had, in a moment of extreme frustration, kicked one of the filing cabinets at work so hard that he had damaged it. This had shocked his colleagues so much that they had reported him to their manager. Jack told me that he was normally a very polite person. In fact, he felt that he was far too polite and compliant most of the time. He said he had been this way since he was a child and that his mother had been quite a commanding person. He just couldn't say 'no' and wanted to please others, so that they would think well of him. The problem was that the more others walked all over him, the more resentful he became, until that moment in the office when he snapped.*

Some of us communicate too passively; others too powerfully. Some of us can also be too critical, whilst others may be too serious when communicating. We communicate with words, yet with face to face communications the words themselves often have less influence than how you say those words or your associated body language. Being aware of our own ways of communicating, and how these can benefit or disadvantage us, can be the key to successful communication.

Also key to communication is the ability to actively listen to others. We spend an enormous amount of time listening, yet we often 'hear' very little. During our day we may spend an hour reading, two hours talking, three hours writing and eight hours listening to colleagues, friends and family, yet at school we spend a lot of time learning to read and write, but less time on learning how to communicate effectively! How often, at home, do we really take the time to listen to our children or partners or are we just often waiting to talk again? To listen to people properly requires our total concentration. It also requires us to set aside our day-to-day preoccupations and worries. If we value someone enough to truly listen to them, they will feel valued and will begin to say valuable things. Since true listening is love in action, nowhere is it more appropriate than within a marriage. Yet many couples rarely truly listen to each other. Time and effort must be set aside for true listening. Our greatest contribution to good communication is responsibility, then comes clarity, focus, non-defensiveness and support.

Ways we speak out

Do you tend to avoid saying what you believe in, or what you want, preferring to compliantly shuffle around in the shadows of other people? Alternatively, do you tend to control the conversation and tell others exactly what you want or believe in, not really considering or caring about what their opinions might be? Through a tool called Transactional Analysis, Eric Berne suggested that there are three main ways that we tend to unconsciously communicate, often developed from childhood. These can be as parent, adult or child type communications depending on the situation.

Sarah came to me looking terribly worried, saying she was having trouble talking to her children's teachers at parents' evenings. When she was at these evenings, she felt like a naughty child being admonished, just as she had been by her own teachers when she was young. I explained to her that this was her adapted child behaviour from her painful childhood experiences. She went on to tell me, looking rather guilty, that when her husband came home late from work she would get very cross with him and tell him off too harshly, which I explained was her critical parent 'teacher like' behaviour coming into play, rather than her normally nurturing warm and loving parent style. Her face then lit up and she said that when she was with her friends she turned into a wonderfully natural, playful, childlike person.

I explained to Sarah the concepts of child, parent and adult communications. I then told her that, based on my experience of her character, she appeared to have a dominant communication style of the nurturing parent and that her childish feelings could easily be overcome. As far as her children's teachers were concerned, she had to remind herself that she was an adult on equal terms with them, rather than allowing them to be the dominant parent to her. She told me that this was easier said than done, which of course is true. By being aware of the three communication styles she was able to begin to consciously communicate in the way she wanted.

The point, therefore, of becoming aware of our different unconscious ways of communicating is to be able to then consciously apply them to situations as we want or need. Lets look more closely at these communication styles as identified by Eric Berne in his book *'Games People Play'* and *'I'm OK, You're OK'* by Thomas Harris

Our child based communications
The child within us represents the child we once were. Within this child is stored all our emotions, all our early experiences, together with our initial view of ourselves and others. Our child ego, which remains with us throughout adulthood, reacts emotionally, with the feelings and instincts of childhood. It has two sides to it: the natural, pre-conditioned child ego and the adapted, rather scary conditioned child ego.

Our natural child ego is primitive, impulsive, spontaneous, instinctive, creative, intuitive and inspirational. Our natural child spreads happiness, warmth and a love of life; we are emotionally beguiling and able to inspire and motivate others. On the downside, however, our natural child ego can also be selfish, thoughtless, undisciplined and demanding. He/she is the un-hurt, unconditioned, wild child such as the one Naomi Wolf described in chapter 4.

Our adapted child ego has adapted to our sense of powerlessness from early childhood. This 'child' can be compliant and 'does as he or she is told', giving rise to guilt, obedience, rebellion or manipulation. We are behaving in an adapted child way when:

- We don't stand up for ourselves, or find that others disregard us
- We don't express our thoughts, feelings and beliefs properly
- We resort to being manipulative instead of expressing ourselves

Are we being polite or just compliant?

Politeness is an expression of good manners and avoids unpleasantness, which is fine as long as we are genuinely behaving according to our own moral code. At its most extreme, it seems that Derrick Bird was a quiet and polite person as supported by friends and family, yet he in May 2010, he went on a shooting spree, in Cumbria, killing both those he apparently held resentments towards as well as then going on to kill a total of 12 innocent people.

Jane came to see me because she was depressed. She had raised her kids whilst also, working part time, so that her husband could devote most of his time to his demanding job. What time he had left was usually spent playing golf or watching the football. Jane didn't question this as her own mother had always put her children and husband before herself. The children, even as adults, still continued to come first and walked all over Jane, which she resented. Also her husband had several affairs, but had always came back full of remorse, telling her how much he loved her. Jane through wanting to care for her family had fallen into the role of subservience.

We looked at how her lack of self-respect seemed to be leading her along a path of frustration and depression. She eventually learnt how to become more assertive with her family, and her children began to respect that she had needs and rights, too. She eventually split from her husband, who told her she had become far too 'aggressive' for him. Sadly many partners see new-found assertiveness as being aggressive.

Our parental based communications

Our parent communication style is based on our parent ego, which has developed from childhood through to adulthood based on mainly observing our parents or other authority figures such as teachers. We can still, therefore, have a parent ego whether we have children or not. This parent ego also has two sides to it: our lovely caring *nurturing parent and* our rather scary *controlling parent.* Our controlling parent can become so furious with neighbouring children, if they are playing noisily, that we may aggressively tell them off. Our nurturing parent, may however, instead gently suggest that these children make less noise. As adults, we can unconsciously adopt either or both of these styles of communication as the situation arises.

Our caring/nurturing parent is kind and protective, attending to the needs of their family. We are communicating in a caring/nurturing parental way when:-

- We can act in a way that respects the rights of another.
- We can express our thoughts, feelings and beliefs in ways, that respect the thoughts, feelings and beliefs of others.
- We consider others' needs as much as our own.

Our controlling parent is a more aggressive or bullying personality type. We might communicate in a controlling parental way when:-

- We act in a way that disrespects the rights of another.
- We express our thoughts, feelings and beliefs in controlling or aggressive ways, even though we may honestly believe our views to be right.

*****Bill** came to my consulting room reluctantly. His wife was threatening to leave him, and even report him to the police, if he* *didn't address his aggression and violence towards her. He was devastated at her lack of loyalty to him and could not initially see how he had done anything wrong. His dad had always ruled the house and told his mother that she needed a slap occasionally to calm her down. He was the boss and that was that. His dad was a manager of a car assembly line and he seemed to get what he wanted in life.*

During our sessions, we looked at how, as a child, we learn our behaviour, usually from our parents. We also examined the effect that his rough behaviour towards his wife and children was having on them. Together we devised ways in which he could 'get what he wanted' through negotiation, rather than a ruling hand.

Our assertively adult based communications
Logical and objective facts, based on unemotional, learnt experiences and common sense, are considered to be part of our adult ego. Our adult ego is therefore the mature and deliberating part of our personality. Our actions and words are unemotional, sensible and well-considered. Our adult ego collects information, evaluates it, works out probabilities, tackles and solves problems, all in a logical, calm, collected manner. Assertive communications are normally based on this adult ego state.

We are communicating in an assertively adult way when:

- We are our own judge and decide for ourselves what we will and will not do
- We are confident enough to change our minds or admit to making mistakes
- We have our own opinions, but also respect the opinions of others
- We can listen attentively as well as speaking up for ourselves
- We can allow silence as a chance to think creatively about other options
- We can clarify to get to the most important issues
- We can show understanding of other people's emotions and reactions

Assertiveness skills need to be learned and practised. Individuals may believe that becoming assertive means becoming selfish, which is partly true, as long as they still consider the feelings of others. Oscar Wilde worded this perfectly:

'A red rose is not selfish because it wants to be a red rose. It would be horribly selfish if it wanted all the other flowers in the garden to be both red and roses.'

10 tips for successful communications

Over many years of helping my clients improve their communications, I have found ten simple tips most useful, which I have summarized below.

1. Active listening and clarity
Active listening is the key to successful communications.

2. Being aware of our egos when we speak out
Recognising our own and others' ego states and communication styles helps us to understand ours and other's emotional reactions to communications.

3. Managing our emotions for clear messages
Sometimes we can fail to maintain good communications because we feel hurt or offended by the message.

At this time it is, therefore, important to consider:

- How we feel wronged and what caused it?
- Was the message justified?
- Is there a pattern to these feelings of hurt or offence?

Remember that the faster our negative emotions rises and the higher it goes, the less it has to do with the immediate situation but has more to do with previous (usually early) experiences.

4. Using appropriate humour

Humour is one of the most useful ways of calming or diffusing fraught communications, provided it is done properly.

5. Using our body language

It is not just the words that are important for communications but also the manner in which you say them and your non-verbal communications. Tone of voice, fluency, posture and movements, physical distance and eye contact are all crucial to good communications.

6. Adapting our appearance

Appearance can be crucial to successful communications. Our clothing, hairstyle and accessories are all important in order to show either an assertive/authoritative confident look or a more approachable relaxed look. Or they can show us to be sloppy or lazy.

7. Accepting and learning from feedback

Positive feedback, as a communication tool is a lovely way of reinforcing preferred behaviour. Negative feedback or criticism, if given appropriately can also help us learn from our mistakes.

8. Negotiating a win-win situation when we speak

When having differing opinions with someone it is easy to get caught up with wanting a win-lose or a right-wrong outcome. Both parties, however, have a unique and valid perspective on life and are not, therefore, necessarily right or wrong.

9. Taking responsibility for yourself

Blame is a very destructive tool to employ in an argument, and is often used as a method of displacing the responsibility from oneself onto others. Remember that, when you point your finger at someone, there is one finger pointing to them and three fingers pointing back towards yourself. So if possible try not to make assumptions, second-guess or mind read.

10. Being true to yourself and your message

This is the most crucial tool for effective and successful communication. We need to be true to ourselves, authentic or congruent. Being professional, objective, non-defensive and non-judgemental with our communications gives us the best chance for success. And never forget that warmth, compassion and generosity can pave the way for the best communications.

10. Screw it - Let's do it. The secret to success

Success

He has achieved success, who has lived well, laughed often, and loved much;

Who has enjoyed the trust of pure women, the respect of intelligent men and the love of little children;

Who has filled his niche and accomplished his task;

Who has never lacked appreciation of Earth's beauty or failed to express it;

Who has left the world better than he found it,

Whether an improved poppy, a perfect poem, or a rescued soul;

Who has always looked for the best in others and given them the best he had;

Whose life was an inspiration;

Whose memory a benediction.

Bessie Anderson Stanley (1904)\

Many people believe that success is about winning, recognition and prosperity. Eckhart Tolle says,

'You cannot become successful you can only be successful in that moment with a quality in what you do, even the most simple action. When doing becomes infused with the timeless quality of Being, that is success'.

There is this guy who lives on a beach near where I live. He occasionally sleeps in a small fishing bunker. He swims each day in the sea and helps the fishmonger out occasionally when he needs it. He takes in the sunshine and he chats to local passers by. He knows everyone and everyone knows him. He loves life and always has a huge smile on his face and seems to appreciate all that life gives him. He earns enough money to go to Thailand and do the same thing in the winter. He seems to have learnt the art of being content with nature and human warmth, without the need to surround himself with material objects or achievements or money to make him happy. Now to be able to do that would mean success to me.

Perhaps that is not your definition of a successful life, but hopefully by now you may want to be successful, in your own way, so that on your epitaph you can truly say that you have Dared to have Lived, Loved and Laughed.

Some of you may have your goals in place by now, as well as the faith and skills to pursue them. But are you still maybe wondering how successful you will be at achieving them? How often have you set your New Year's resolutions then given them up a few weeks later? What about the diet that never quite got to the goal weight? What about all those projects that you started that are still hanging around unfinished? You may have enough motivation and effort to get within reach of your goals, but then life and obstacles take over and motivation dwindles. So what will make you succeed this time? Well I hope it is going to be reading this chapter! Here is a man, whom I believed achieved his goals for success:

__Harry__ loved life and was one determined elderly man, who had always achieved his goals on the many projects he had set himself during his lifetime. His critical goal, this time, was to continue to live life well, despite facing life-threatening heart problems. Coming up to age 80 he began to feel continually tired and out of breath. He wondered if this was just old age creeping up on him. He couldn't walk very far and settled for watching more TV. Then, on one of his regular walks, he collapsed and was taken to hospital. After tests they found out that he had an aneurism (a thinning of one of the main arteries leading to his heart). Harry was also told that he had severely blocked arteries, which would require a triple heart bypass operation to repair it. The heart consultants told him that they were very concerned about carrying out either operation as, at his age, it could trigger a serious stroke. They told him that, if he was careful, there was a good chance his aneurism could last a few more years without bursting. Also that he was unlikely to have a heart attack if he took life easy and didn't get too excited.

Harry returned from this consultation devastated, as he had always been someone who took life by the horns and enjoyed every moment of it. Excitement and passion were an integral part of his life. He could not envisage just living an idle bland life, with the fear of being too active or excited lest it might kill him. He became quite low and said that he would rather die than live what he perceived to be 'a living death'. He had always been a bit of a gambler, working for the Tote bookmakers, for most of his life, and he decided that he wanted to take up the ultimate gamble i.e. with his life. He called up his consultants and told them that he wanted to have both operations, accepting the risks of having a stroke or dying. One month later, Harry undertook a six-hour operation, where two surgeons did their separate procedures at the same time. His gamble paid off and he did not suffer a stroke, although he was extremely poorly after the surgery. But by the time he has reached his next birthday, a month later, he was feeling much better and he enjoyed a huge family party. Although he was not quite dancing yet, he was chatting away and drinking champagne.

Six months after that party, having worked hard on his rehabilitation, Harry's energy and mobility increased to such a level that he was able to go on long walks. His daughter had pre-booked a box at Ascot and told him that it would be used as a celebration of life whether he was alive or dead. As it happens it was a glorious day of celebration, with him as the star guest. He says he feels as if he has had a second chance at life and loves every minute of it. He had always been quite a gentle, unassertive man, but he decided, this time round, that he would make more of an effort to embrace life and do all those things that he had always wanted to do but never quite had time for. He now goes to bridge three times a week, he has his daily walk and goes on regular cruises. Unfortunately just as he became more healthy, his wife became quite infirm and dependent upon him. Despite being her carer, he still goes to all the parties he is invited to and recently threw his own party. Why? Because it was spring! He has also been able to do odd jobs around the house for his daughters once again. From that he regained a huge sense of achievement and self-respect.

This particular case study, is the case of my own father's experience, He is now aged 88 and is fit and healthy. He even danced the foxtrot, the tango and the jive with me on a weekend away and is looking forward to going to America to his grandsons wedding!

Let us look at how we can guarantee our own success.

10 tips to ensure success

1. Success through SMART goals
Like Harry, if we wish to succeed with our goals, we must make sure our goals are SMART:
S–specific   **M**–measurable   **A**–agreed/attainable
R – realistic   **T** – time bound

- **Specific** goals direct attention and activity towards the specific tasks e.g. Weight loss

- **Measurable** goals help to direct effort towards achievement e.g. lose 5kg
- **Attainable** goals help build the persistence required for achievement e.g. 5kg is attainable for most people
- **Realistic** goals result in less anxiety, more motivation, and more chance of success e.g. I am over two stone overweight but realistically 5kg is all I can lose for the moment.
- **Time bound** goals, within the individuals control are more achievable e.g. lose 5kg over the next two months

2. Success through overcoming obstacles and fear

Obstacles and challenges in life, can stop us achieving our goals. By now you may be aware of your own obstacles and how to overcome them. Obstacles can be psychological as well as physical. These are largely due to our conditioning as a child, when we were told, *'Don't do that', 'Be careful', ' 'What will others think?'* and so on so that they create a fear within ourselves. Some may be simple and others much more complicated. For the complicated ones, consult a trusted relative, a friend or a counsellor as a way of untangling them so they can become achievable.

Eckhart Tolle explains that when you are present, when your attention is fully in the Now, that Presence will flow into and transform what you do. There will be quality and power in it. You are present when what you are doing is not primarily a means to an end (money, prestige, winning) but fulfilling in itself, when there is joy and aliveness in what you do. And, of course, you cannot be present unless you become friendly with the present moment. That is the basis for effective action, uncontaminated by negativity.

Don't, therefore, be too despondent if you seem, initially, to have a lot of obstacles to overcome. Just tackle each one gradually. Like the saying, 'How do you eat an elephant?' One bite at a time (Bill Hogan). Look at these commonplace obstacles that I have come across in my work with clients, and some practical tips for overcoming them.

	Obstacle	How I will overcome it
What is stopping you from moving to the location you prefer?		
	I can't afford to move yet	Save for when you can move
What is stopping you from doing what you want?		
At work:	I can't find a good job	Look at the job market or retrain
At home:	I have no energy left for me	Doing things you love creates energy
At play:	I have no time for fun.	Make time for fun by cutting out less important things

What is stopping you from being with whom you would like to be with?

Partner:	I can't find the right person	Feel right within yourself first
Family:	I feel suffocated by family	Make strong boundaries between you and your family
Friends:	I am too shy to socialise	Join some networking sites or clubs
Community:	No one needs my help	Help is always needed and you can do it

What is stopping you from being the person you would like to be?

In your body:	I have no time for exercise	Get up earlier and run/exercise in the park
In your mind:	I feel negative/fearful/angry	Seek help to become more positive or less afraid or angry

What is stopping you from having your finances straight?

	I'm hopeless with money	Seek advice from a financial adviser or debt counsellor.

3. Success through motivation and rewards

The psychologist Benjamin Bloom has said that it is drive and determination, not great talent, which leads to success. The Dalai Lama says that 'higher goals' such as kindness, compassion and spiritual development lead to happiness. He says this is linked to developing determination and enthusiasm. Effort, he says, is the final factor that brings about change.

What motivates us to really succeed?
Most of us probably don't even think about our primary motives, which are based on biological survival needs. We may be more aware of our secondary motives which are based on our social needs - wanting n to be loved or to belong to groups: religious, work, social, family, gangs or political. We also want to feel loved, needed and accepted by others.

Then we have our esteem and self-actualisation needs. There are two types of esteem. The first is self-esteem, which is the confidence and ability to value and believe in ourselves. Secondly, we have attention and recognition needs, which we look to get from other people. Self-actualisation is when we truly maximise our potential. At this level, we can expect to feel intense feelings of happiness, and a sense of harmony and well-being.

Sheena had been through a lot during her life. She had been a highly motivated young career woman and had met the man of her dreams, whom she felt very happy with. She also maintained good relationships with her family and friends.

Although she had never felt very confident at school, after university she got a good management job, which had increased her self-esteem greatly. She was then promoted and recognised for the competent person she obviously was. Throughout her twenties she had fun, worked hard and was well paid. Sheena and her husband eventually decided to have children and she left work to face the new challenge of being a mother. She realised, soon after the birth of her first child, that she could not convert her competent management skills to parenting, and began to feel very unhappy. Her self-esteem plummeted and she became quite depressed.

Through therapy she began to understand more about herself and how she related to her partner and her children. She wanted to work, at least on a part-time basis, in order to fulfil her need for recognition and respect, and for her to be able to value herself. She retrained in a more flexible caring profession – a career that she had always wanted but had never felt clever enough to pursue. She also learnt how to become more selfish and assertive. As her children grew, Sheena also grew in strength and wisdom, becoming more content with herself and her life. To this day, she continues to develop herself, both professionally and personally. Fun, love, connection, compassion and effort, she believes, are the essential oils to lubricate successful and happy human living. She still comes back to me once a year for her psychological MOT and tells me that she is happier than she ever dreamt possible.

Rewards
Athletes go to phenomenal lengths to win at their chosen sport. To win, not only do they have to be physically fit, they must also be motivated and have the right mindset. The list that follows is an amalgam of rewards that the coaches of international athletes give to motivate their protégés:

- Regular use of individual rewards, based on what they value, contingent on performance.
- Rewards given as soon after success as possible.
- Rewards and praise given sincerely, enthusiastically and repeatedly.
- Encouragement from others (team members, friends, colleagues) for good performance.
- Rewards not only for winning, but also for personal bests

4. Success through self-belief and positivity
We have already seen that some people always seem to get to where they want to be, seemingly without even trying, whilst others just can't get their act together. What is it that makes the second type of person find life so difficult? One of the main factors is low self-esteem which is a combination of self doubt and low confidence - that loud voice in

their head saying: I'm not much fun to be with; I would like to be someone else; I often make a mess of my life; I am not as attractive as most people; I am often critical of what I am doing; I often feel negative about my life and am a half-empty person; I never seem to get my act together at work or at home or I feel shy and would prefer to stay in than meet new people. The person with high self-belief seems to get what they want in life, whilst the self-doubter often loses out. Which do you think you are?

Self-believing behaviour:	**Self-doubting behaviour:**
A self believer always makes time to achieve their goals	A self doubter is always too busy to achieve their goals
A self believer deals with the problems of each day as it comes	A self doubter goes around the problem or leaves it for tomorrow
A self believer keeps to a commitment	A self doubter makes excuses
A self believer listens carefully	A self doubter waits to talk
A self believer learns from others	A self doubter pretends to know
A self believer is responsible for themselves	A self doubter blames others
A self believer focuses on solutions	A self doubter focuses on problems.

If you still believe you are a self-doubter with low self esteem then go back and re-read Chapter 1 to help you build your self belief and confidence.

Turning our negative beliefs into positive beliefs
So many of us have been programmed to believe that:

- I must be accepted and loved and if I am not, life will be awful and unbearable
- I must get what I want in life and if I don't then it will be awful and unbearable
- Life must be easy, painless and happy - if it isn't, then it will be awful and unbearable
- Life must continue until its natural end at a very old age

Once we accept that the above is not guaranteed, then we can begin to develop the patience to face the challenges that are presented to us, to enjoy the moments of happiness that we receive, and to accept the inevitable losses that arise out of being human, particularly the ultimate loss of death, which is as natural to life as birth is.

Sheena realised that in order for her to attain the happiness and success she wanted in her life, she had to re-programme many of her negative beliefs. For example she realised that being right and wrong were not absolutes but just differing perspectives. She also realised that marriage was not to be held onto at all costs. She changed her negative beliefs to the following:

- I would like to be loved, but can only achieve this through genuinely loving others.
- Although it would be nice to get what I want all the time, I realise that this is not always possible and that I must be patient enough to work towards eventually attaining the things that I want from life. Some things I must accept that I may never get.
- Life cannot always be painless, happy and certain. I will have moments of pain, moments of disappointment and moments of happiness.
- Unfortunately life does not always continue to its natural end. Although the untimely death of a loved one causes much sadness and pain, if I accept that death is as much a natural part of our existence as birth is, then I can hope eventually to enjoy my life without my lost loved one.
- What negative beliefs might you have that you would like to re-programme? Tick any from above and think about what other negative beliefs you might have. Then think about what impact those beliefs have on you and if you want to re-programme them then do it now!

5. Success through listening to your own soul through coincidences and intuition

Coincidences pull us towards some special destiny. Coincidence is the gift of insight not sought for, and it is up to us whether we use this insight or not. Carl Jung called this perception of meaningful coincidence 'Synchronicity', which he described as being a universal law, which operated to help move humans on towards greater growth in consciousness. Being in the right place at the right time may ensure we follow a particular career, or accidentally meet someone who becomes very significant in our life. The biggest challenge is whether we decide to listen to those coincidences, or whether we dismiss them. Worse still, we may miss them, because we are too busy focussing on what others say or our own habits, goals and visions.

Intuitive messages from the night - many people get very frustrated if they wake up in the middle of the night thinking about a dream they have just had, or thoughts that keep coming into their mind. Some see this merely as losing valuable sleep, with the possibility of being tired and irritable the next day. I see these moments in the middle of the night as a wonderful opportunity to listen to my own intuition and I keep a notebook by my bed for writing down important things. At that time of night, our egos are often sleeping, while intuition is awake. Like Jung, I believe that we are all guided by our unconscious minds and that these minds are not only a huge store of current life data but also contain past life or even universal data. Within this store, therefore, we have a vast database of information that we can draw on to help guide us through life. We just have to discover our own personal methods of retrieving it. Instead of dismissing these unconscious intuitive thoughts, take a notebook and write them down.

There are many ways, other than dreams or midnight thoughts, of taking time out to listen to coincidence or to listen to one's inner thoughts. I find I often get inspiration while driving my car or doing some other repetitive task, like gardening or working out at the gym. Repetitive cognitive or physical tasks, through neuro-linguistic processes, somehow quieten the logical left-brain ego and allow the unconscious thoughts of the creative right brain to come through. Meditation, yoga or hypnosis also help to quieten our ego, allowing our unconscious thoughts to emerge. The more we practise these techniques, the more easily our unconscious thoughts will emerge.

It is important that you choose your own way to find your unconscious soul guidance, and to keep an eye out for powerful coincidences. If you then proceed with a certain amount of discipline, bypassing your old patterns, you can begin to fully integrate your new spiritual self into your day-to-day life, even under the most stressful situations. Then you can become less 'bovvered' about what others think.

'Am I bovvered' attitude
Remember that great sketch when Catherine Tate says in a cockney accent. Am I bovvered?

How many of us really can say that we aren't bovvered about what others think?

- Am I bovvered if others are envious of me or my successes?
  Bothered enough to become a shadow of these people instead of the guiding light?
- Am I bovvered if I don't live up to my parents or others expectations?
  Bothered enough to keep pushing myself to 'achieve' to live up to them?
- Am I bovvered if I am not keeping at the same pace as others?
  Bothered enough to follow their pace rather than stick to what I feel comfortable with?
- Am I bovvered if I fail at something?
  Bothered enough to constantly berate myself for my failures?

The last one is the most difficult one to kick, so perhaps you can tell yourself, 'I am not bovvered by failure as long as I can learn from it'. Remember that successful people are not those who have never failed but those who have failed plenty of times and who have chosen to learn from their failures. Caring about oneself as well as others is extremely important, but not being bothered so much about what other people say or think is also important.

6. Success through patience
Patience is a virtue that very few of us have, particularly when we are young and exuberant. Today we live in a world, which enables us to have things now.

Through the internet we can get instant credit, instant knowledge, instant purchases, instant viewing of media and even instant relationships. So why do we need patience? Patience, to me, is something that develops with maturity. It is the wisdom to know when to wait for the right time for things to happen. It is the faith to know that if we continue to follow the path that our heart takes us, then everything will unfold and success will be achieved. It may not be the success that you had originally envisaged for yourself, which may have been wealth, instant love or happiness or an easy life. Instead, it may be success in terms of achieving true contentment and a deeper love and the glorious feeling of being authentic – being true to one's soul.

Peter, age 52, had always been an extremely ambitious and gregarious sort of chap. He was a bit of a lad with the girls and as a youth had been extremely rebellious and was always getting into trouble of one sort or another. He married when he got tired of his youthful exploits and felt he needed stability and to settle down, but he never felt really in love. He did, however, have three wonderful children, whom he loved very much. He had had a life full of set backs as well as successes. He had broken his back twice, once as a young man, which left him with a slight arthritic condition, but this had not deterred him from building a successful building and property company. He lived the high life and enjoyed every minute of it, except for the fact that he was becoming more and more

distant from his wife. He broke his back for the second time due
to a serious car accident. He was relieved that he had not been
left paralysed, but he was in terrible pain, which he has suffered
from ever since. He had to give up work for a couple of years and
his building company folded, although he was determined to
pay most people back. He sold his large property and everything
else he had and bought a smaller home for his family. He and
his wife eventually split up. He felt he had truly hit rock bottom
and became quite depressed.

Peter realised that he had to do something with his life. He
found some continuous strong pain medication patches, which
helped his pain management considerably. He was given the
chance to take over a roadside burger bar, which he worked at
building up very much. He joined an internet dating site and
found the woman of his dreams. He told me that he had had it
all at one time - money, health, youth and the high life – but had
never felt truly happy. Now, although he has very little material
wealth and is in constant pain, whilst working hard selling
burgers he says that he much prefers the simpler more authentic
lifestyle that he has now. He loves his work and all the people he
meets whom he serves. He has also given himself permission to
play more. Everyone goes there not just for the burgers, but for
the smile on his face and the laughs they have together. He goes
on exciting holidays with his girlfriend and has learnt to dance
and ski for the first time in his life. He doesn't feel that he has
to have material ambitions any more, but instead enjoys simply
being. He still has his true friends, his wonderful children and
as well as finding love.

7. Success through opening up your heart to love and happiness

It is only through opening up your heart to love others that we can find true happiness and success in our lives. We looked at the relationship between Jan and Ed in chapter 3.

Jan, having divorced her husband said that it had been tough initially being single but that she had eventually found herself - and she loved what she saw. At last she loved and accepted herself totally. She found a beautiful home by the sea where she felt supremely happy, calm and comfortable. She renovated and furnished her home lovingly with creativity and to her own taste. She became more connected with her friends and family than she had ever been whilst married and threw parties, went on singles holidays and had plenty of fun.

Jan started eating healthily and employed a personal trainer to help her to exercise regularly. She took up yoga with friends, which normally ended up with a few drinks, fun and laughter. She even told me that on a recent activity holiday she had performed the trapeze! Not bad for a woman in her 50s, she said. Having been single for a number of years, she said that she had been feeling doubtful that she would ever find a guy who would love and cherish her just for being her. But through internet dating she found such a lovely man. Then, unexpectedly, a rescue dog entered her life. She has since taken him out for long walks along the sea front and played with him and talked freely with other dog lovers and walkers. She discovered the immense, unconditional love that a dog can give, and the love that she was able to give back. She also realised that, whilst she still has tmany things in her life she wanted to do, there would be further challenges she would have to meet. Also for her to accept love and happiness, she also has to accept the possibility of loss and suffering. I was happy that Jan had not only found herself, but in doing so had found love. Like Alan Watts had stated – Jan was not just a separate ego housed in a bag of skin, but connected to a wonderful world of beautiful physical objects and loving people.

8. Success through managing your changes

People often want to make positive changes in their lives, or engage in healthier behaviours, but are prevented from doing so by encountering a sort of inertia or resistance within themselves. Maybe this is because we simply become habituated or accustomed to doing things in certain ways. And then we become lazy, doing only the things we like to do, or are used to doing. We then have to make a supreme effort to establish new behavioural patterns. By making that steady effort, however, we *can* eventually overcome any form of negative conditioning and make positive changes in our lives. If we look at this picture of the cycle of change, which is used by many substance abuse rehabilitation programmes, we will see the various stages:

Cycle of change

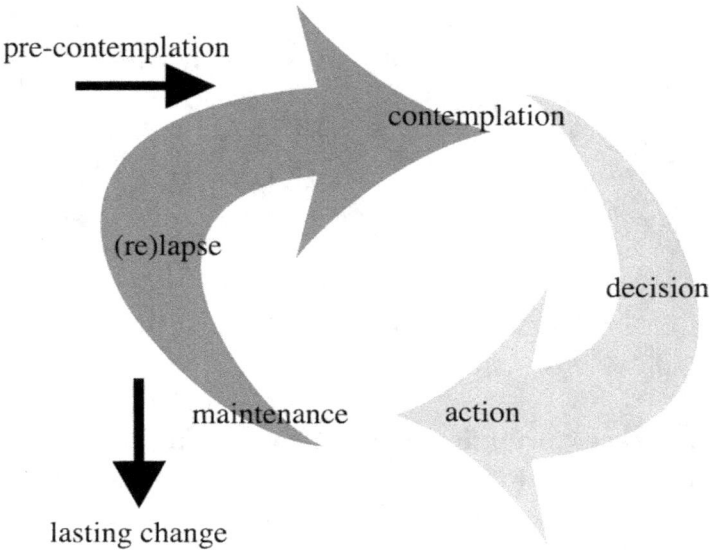

Contemplation - At this stage the change has not happened, but gradually we begin to understand how negative emotions and behaviours are harmful to our pursuit of happiness. However, at this stage we may employ many excuses for putting off the change.

Decision - This is an important stage, as the decision is what brings on action for change. Planning and setting start dates for action is essential for kicking off on the right track.

Action to carry out a change - This part is the most exciting. Beginning a new diet or exercise programme, or telling everyone that you have quit smoking or embarked on another new change in your life, is a very positive experience. We feel centre stage and others are desperate to support us in our goals. Our determination is still bubbling and we are carried along by our adrenaline for action.

Maintenance of a change - Things may be going well for a while, but maintaining it becomes hard work. We miss the habit and enjoyment of eating, smoking, drinking alcohol, taking drugs, or whatever habit we are attempting to leave behind. We may be getting fed up with our personal trainer, who just keeps shouting at us to keep pumping the iron. Other people have lost interest in supporting us. A realistic attitude and a large amount of effort is, therefore, what is required to sustain the change we have begun.

Relapse is a normal part of change. We are human after all. We get fed up and bored with the effort of our new routine. So we let go of it for a while, but hopefully return to the grind of the maintenance stage. But that period of relapse can get longer and longer, so that it is more and more difficult to get back on track, and we may have to start the whole cycle again.

9. Success through Searching Deep Inside Yourself

In order to achieve your goals and find success it is essential to *'Search deep inside yourself'*. Yoga teaches you that you can stretch your body far more than you think you can, with the right focus and breathing. Human beings generally fulfil just a fraction of their potential, and seem to be satisfied with that. A small minority of people, however, search deep inside themselves and go for challenges that take them to the limits of their potential.

A friend of mine, Jane, annually runs the London Marathon. She is a very focused person and has faced many challenges in her life, as well as having been tremendously successful in business. A few years ago she faced some tough personal challenges when her aunt, who looked after her blind mother, died. She then had to take over the day to day care of her mother. Jane decided that she wanted to beat her personal best in the London Marathon and employed a trainer to help her to achieve this. She also became Trustee of a wonderful charity called 'Dreams Come True', and is sponsored to raise money for it with each marathon she runs. This is what she said about what drives her to continue running marathons:

'Those who know me well will be aware that one of the things that keeps me putting one foot in front of the other for 26 miles is the thought of a glass of champagne at the end of it... Those of you who know me better will know that while champagne helps, what actually keeps me going for those 26 miles - and all the hard training miles that go before it - is the power of my own crazy dreams. When things get tough, or when life throws a tough number your way, having a dream is sometimes the only thing that can help you hang in and press on. I am now a Trustee of the 'Dreams Come True' Charity and have seen first hand how much of a difference that fulfilling a dream can make to a child with a life-threatening or terminal illness. Experiencing a dream fulfilled can not only bring real joy into children's lives, but also a new focus that can enable a family to see beyond the endless rounds of hospital appointments and the relentless difficulties of coping with serious illness and help them find the positives and the will to carry on.

Due to an injury Jane didn't achieve her personal best that year but she raised nearly £5000 for **'Dreams Come True'**. She still aims to achieve that personal best and raise more money for her charity. For the rest of us, who do our bit, it does not always need to be so much of a challenge. This poem seems particularly pertinent to Jane.

Dare to Dream, Dare to be Different C. W. Longenecker

If you think you are better, you are
If you like to win, but think you can't
It is almost certain you won't
If you think you'll lose, you're lost
For out of the world we find
Success begins with a fellows will
It is all in the state of mind

If you think you're outclassed, you are
You've got to think high to rise,
You've got to be sure of yourself before
You can ever win a prize
Life's battles don't always go
To the stronger or faster man
But soon or later the man who wins
Is the man WHO THINKS HE CAN

10. Success through seeking support from positive mentors

This is probably the most important factor towards success. Without a positive mentor, who is someone who believes in you wholeheartedly and yet who is able to positively criticise you and help you grow, then you are lost. Everybody, however positive they are, can have dark and and negative days when they stop believing in themselves and want to revert back their old ways.

Do you know someone who understands you and who encourages you to fulfil your dreams and unlock your potential? They are your best support system. If not look at the people around you for such positive support. As you may have guessed by now until Jenny's death I was lucky enough to have a person like this. Since her death there have been others whom I have found along the way both professionally and personally who have believed and helped me towards success.

Alternatively there are those in the media who can help us stay motivated towards success. There are great websites like www.ted.com, where significant people comment with their wise words or motivating books such as these below.

Let us finally look at what some successful people say about success

'Screw it - let's do it!' What Richard Branson, founder of Virgin

'When I was starting out in life, things were more certain than they are these days. You had a career lined up, often the same one your father followed. Most mothers stayed at home. Today nothing is sure, and life is one long struggle. People have to make choices if they are to get anywhere. The best lesson I learned was to just do it.

It doesn't matter what it is, or how hard it might seem, as the ancient Greek, Plato said, 'The beginning is the most important part of any work'. A journey of a thousand miles starts with that first step. If you look ahead to the end, and all the weary miles between, with all its dangers you might face, you might never take that first step. And whatever it is you want to achieve in life, if you don't make the effort you won't reach your goal. So take the first step. There will be many challenges. You might get knocked back - but in the end, you will make it. The staff at Virgin have a name for me. It is Dr 'Yes'. They call me this because I won't say no. I find more reasons to do things than not to do them. I will never say, 'I can't do this because I don't know how to'. I will give it a go. I won't let silly rules stop me. My motto is 'Screw it – let's do it!'

'How to Change Your Life in 7 Steps', *John Bird*, **founder of** *'The Big Issue' and author of* **says follow the 3% rule for success**

John Bird, in contrast to Richard Branson, was born into a London Irish family in a slum-ridden part of Notting Hill, just after the Second World War. He was homeless at five and in an orphanage between seven and ten. From ten onwards he was shop-lifting, burgling houses and generally stealing whatever he could lay his hands on. In his late twenties, after several prison sentences, John became involved in politics.

He also fathered three children, became a printer and successfully ran his own business. At the age of 45, his many life experiences enabled him to start the production of the Big Issue. He strongly believes in the 3% rule. That is, to set goals and a series of steps to get you there, but remember to only start with 3% and it doesn't matter if you only move slowly. As long as you are not standing completely still you are on your way. Then enjoy and celebrate your gains, no matter how small.

Together, with a common purpose of love and peace, we can be amazingly powerful

'Ancient Chinese proverb. A little bit of fragrance always clings onto the hand that gives the roses. When you work to improve the lives of others, you indirectly elevate your own life in the process. When you practice acts of kindness daily, your own life becomes far richer and more meaningful. To cultivate the sacredness and sanctity of each day serve others in some way.'

Emily Craddock, whom I have mentioned throughout this book, had her own vision of a perfect world. She summarized this vision, within an interview for an American TV channel, just before she drowned whilst on a Greenpeace expedition in the Amazon. I have added some possible action points of my own in brackets:

- ***There are too many people in the world.*** *The world needs to stop making so many babies. (e.g.* supporting agencies that help promote family planning)
- ***I would like to see an end to large, multi-national corporations running the world*** (e.g. buying more fair trade products, rather than buying from the multi-nationals.)
- ***The UN as a proper world government with powers*** (e.g. ensuring that the UN has the proper powers to be able to promote world peace)
- ***More respect for nature and for each other*** (e.g. Looking after our beautiful planet; going to green gyms; supporting agencies such as Greenpeace who put pressure on governments to take action to reduce dangerous Emissions; recycling and not wasting energy, while promoting sustainable energy.)
- ***A bit more humanity and a bit less greed*** A bit less desire for the latest Nintendo and the biggest car and the nicest house and more consideration for that guy on the street down there. It might be his fault that he is a drunk guy on the street, but he is still a human being. (e.g. we could keep our cars longer or even let them go in favour of buying an eco friendly car or using a bicycle or walking. We could empathise more with those people in the world who are much less fortunate than ourselves. Those who experience extreme poverty, who are experiencing an abuse of human rights,

who are dying of Aids or starvation, who are involved in bloody warfare or who are victims of the ever increasing ecological disasters)

We are incredible even as individual human beings, with a huge edge over the rest of the creatures on this planet in that we can plan, we can reason, we can invent and we can recreate our selves. But if instead of seeing this world as Alan Watts says as 'Black versus White', as separate polar entities that must be conquered e.g. light versus darkness, good versus bad, life versus death, one individual against another or one nation or race versus another, we see ourselves as part of a connected world then, perhaps, we can have the strength of one race – The Human Race.

Together, as a community of beautiful, authentic, loving, caring people, and with a common purpose of love and peace, we can be amazingly powerful. Much more powerful than any government that currently exists. We are the world and we just need to realise it and harness the amazing power of the Internet to get together, speak out and take action to do something about the ecological and population problems we face.

If we can listen to our souls when there is the next ecological disaster, then we may not judge the country, where the disaster has happened, for its politics or its past. But instead connect with our human compassion for those survivors who are homeless because of it, injured, bereft and without food or drink. If it was us in this situation, what would we wish others to do? Our ecology and climate are in a state of flux and it will not go away unless as a global world we all do something about it.

Remember John Lennon's words in his song:

Imagine – John Lennon

Imagine there's no heaven. It's easy if you try.
No hell below us, above us only sky
Imagine all the people living for today...
Imagine there's no countries, it isn't hard to do.
Nothing to kill or die for and no religion too. Imagine
all the people living life in peace....
You may say I'm a dreamer, but I'm not the only one.
I hope someday you'll join us and the world will be as one
Imagine no possessions, I wonder if you can.
No need for greed or hunger. A brotherhood of man
Imagine all the people sharing all the world...
You may say I'm a dreamer, but I'm not the only one.
I hope someday you'll join us and the world will live as one

I wish you success with daring to live, love and be happy and leave you with this final quote from Nelson Mandela, the man who could move nations into compassion and action, through his love for his people, his passion for justice and equality, his determination and his patience to continue with his work despite being incarcerated in prison for many years.

Our deepest fear is not that we are inadequate. Our deepest fear is that we are powerful beyond measure. It is our light not our darkness that most frightens us. We ask ourselves: Who am I to be brilliant, gorgeous, talented and fabulous: Actually, who are you not to be? You are a child of God. Your playing small doesn't serve the world. There is nothing enlightened about shrinking so other people won't feel insecure around you. We are born to manifest the glory of God that is within us. It's not just in some of us; its in everyone. And as we let our own light shine, we unconsciously give other people permission to do the same. As we are liberated from our own fear our presence automatically liberates others. Nelson Mandela 'Make sure that you have fun while you are advancing along the path of your goals and purpose. Never forget the importance of living with unbridled exhilaration. Never neglect to see the exquisite beauty in all living things. Remain joyful, spirited and curious. Stay focused on your life's work and on giving selfless service to others and let the universe take care of everything else. Keep passion at the forefront of your mind. A burning sense of passion is the most potent fuel for your dreams' The Monk Who Sold His Ferrari – Robin Sharma

Bibliography

Berne, Eric '**Games People Play**' (1964) Ballantine books. New York

Bird, John *How to Change your Life in 7 Steps* (2008) Vermilion. London

Branson, Richard *Screw it - let's do it!* (2008) Vermilion, London

Cleese, John/Skynner, Robin, *Families and How to Survive Them'*(1989) Manderin Paperbacks. London.

Cockcroft, George *The Dice Man* (1999) Harper Collins, London

Cooper, Cary, Cooper, Rachel, Eaker, Lynn. *Living with Stress* (1988) Penguin. London

Dalai Lama/Cutler Howard, *The Art of Happiness* (1998) Hodder & Staughton.London

Emsley, John, *The Consumer's Good Chemical Guide* (1996). Corgi. London.

Eysenk, Michael, *Happiness - Facts and Myths* (1994) Lawrence Erlbaum Associates. Hove

Goldman, Albert, *Elvis* (1984) McGraw Hill. New York

Goleman, Daniel, *Emotional Intelligence* (1996) Bloomsbury, London.

Gray, John, *Men Are From Mars, Women Are From Venus.* (1993) Thorsons, London.

Dr Green, Christopher *Understanding Attention Deficit Disorder* (1995) Vermilion. London

Greenfield, Susan, *The Human Brain, A Guided Tour* (1997)Weidenfeld and Nicolson, London

Hallowell,Edward /Ratey, John *Attention Deficit Disorder* (1996). Fourth Estate.London

Harris, Thomas *I'm OK, You're OK* (1995) Arrow Books. London

Hartley-Brewer, Elizabeth. (1994). *Positive Parenting, Raising Children With Self-Esteem.* Cedar, London

Harrold, *Fiona The 7 Rules of Success* (1988) Hodder & Staughton.London

Huxley, Aldous, *Brave New World* (1932) Flamingo. London.

Kramer, Peter, *Listening to Prozac* (1994) Fourth Estate, London

Lacey, Ron, *The Complete Guide to Pyschiatric Drugs* (1996) Vermillion. London.

Maugham Somerset, *Of Human Bondage* (1915) Bantum Classics. London

McIlveen, Rob & Gross, Richard, *BioPyschology* (1996) Hodder & Stooughton, London.

Nin, Anais *A Woman Speaks* (1975) Penguin. London

Phillips, Adam *Monogamy* (1996) Faber & Faber, London

Pirsig, Robert M, *Zen and the Art of Motorcycle Maintenance (2004). Vintage. London*

Rowe, Dorothy, *Depression, The Way Out of Your Prison* (1983) Routledge, London

Russell, Bertrand, *History of Western Philosophy* (1996). Routledge. London

Scott Peck. *The Road Less Travelled* (1978). Arrow, London.

Sharma, Robin. *The Monk Who Sold His Ferrari* Jaico. India

Tolle, Eckhart. A New Earth (2005), Penguin, London

Watts, Alan *The Book on The Taboo Against Knowing Who You Are* (2009) Souvenir Press. London

Wilde, Oscar *Epigrams of Oscar Wilde* (1996). Senate. London

Williams, Margery *Velveteen Rabbit (1922) Delacorte Press. New York*

Wolf, Naomi, *Fire with Fire (1994). Vintage. London*